D0922845

The Shapes of our Theatre

BOOKS BY JO MIELZINER

The Shapes of Our Theatre
Designing for the Theatre

The Shapes of Our Theatre

by Jo Mielziner

Edited by C. Ray Smith

Clarkson N. Potter, Inc./Publisher NEW YORK

DISTRIBUTED BY CROWN PUBLISHERS, INC.

Library of Congress Catalog Card Number: 70–111343

Manufactured in the United States of America

First Edition

Published simultaneously in Canada by
General Publishing Company Limited

Table of Contents

Author's Note

The illustrations in this book are all schematic plans that emphasize the essential relationship of the two basic areas of a theatre interior—the action area and the audience area. Black triangles represent actors; black rectangles represent audience. In certain periods of princely patronage, royalty is indicated by a star symbol.

Acknowledgments

Primarily, I wish to acknowledge my indebtedness to the Ford Foundation and to the Arts of the Theatre Foundation for generous financial help and encouragement in the writing of this book.

My warmest gratitude also to my editor, C. Ray Smith, to Edward F. Kook for guidance and encouragement, and to Sandra Jean Hance, who aided me in my struggle to turn clear and fervent ideas into written words. On the visual side, I wish to acknowledge the many months of work of my staff in preparing the illustrations. Among these fine craftsmen were: Leor C. Warner III, John H. Döepp, and John A. McGroder, Jr.

Preface

Many citizens of generosity and good will take pride in contributing to the costs of new theatre buildings, and they feel that they are accomplishing something. In most cases they are probably right.

But there is an ambiguity about the meaning of the word "theatre." To most people it means the building in which theatrical performances occur. To professionals it refers to the performance inside the building—the script, the actors, and the scenic design. O'Neill's best plays are "good theatre" because they come to life on the stage. His scripts are only notes for a performance. "Theatre" is a form of incandescence.

For years Jo Mielziner, a gifted artist and scene designer, has been aware of the inadequacies of many theatre buildings to spark the incandescence of "good theatre" on their stages. The buildings may be too large and imposing; the décor may be distracting; the proportions of the stage may be unworkable; the shape of the stage may be uncongenial.

It has always seemed to me that the conventional proscenium stage sets up a competition between the actors and the audience. It divides them into two entities that face each other defiantly, although the proscenium stage is essential to certain kinds of plays, like Restoration comedies. It has always seemed to me that the apron or thrust stage is the most theatrical and inviting, although it makes Restoration comedies diffuse and spiritless. Nothing is ideal for everything.

Jo Mielziner knows more about this problem of form than most people. His comments are searching and illuminating and derive from his combination of artistic imagination and technological exactitude. Since theatres, once built, cannot be altered into other shapes that alter the relationship of the performance to the audience, I think it would be irresponsible to design a new theatre without consulting this book. Architects need it; they lack theatrical experience. For a theatre building can easily become a theatrical liability; it can make it difficult for an audience to enjoy a play.

In an early part of his book Jo Mielziner refers to Lope de Vega's classic statement of the fundamentals of creative theatre: "Give me four trestles, four boards, two actors and a passion." A passion is the first essential; the performance always comes first. We have many more methods, materials, and techniques than Lope de Vega had in the seventeenth century. But the relationship between performance and audience remains the same. Jo Mielziner, a theatre man of wide experience and understanding, has put everything into clear perspective in this admirable book.

BROOKS ATKINSON

The Shapes of our Theatre

I

Introduction

Serious problems are endangering theatre as we have known it, but the notion that it has little place in our day and no hope for the future is unacceptable to me. As a form of communication, theatre is undying. The art of designing buildings for this living theatre is also undying.

This book is about planning and designing the interior shapes of our theatre buildings. The usual dictionary definition of "shape" refers to "external or outward form, configuration or contour." The shape I refer to is strictly that of the theatre building interior. It is a shape that grows out of, and is responsive to, the vital workings of spoken drama.

The theatres I am primarily concerned with are those for spoken drama and comedy and for musical theatre, which is closely related in its needs and requirements. Opera and ballet will be touched upon only to clarify influences and to explain inheritance and traditions.

The shapes of our theatres are vital to the drama they house. It is my belief that new imaginative approaches to our theatre shapes must be developed and astutely investigated. Such new approaches will create a richer, more effective, and more relevant atmosphere for the theatre, extend its audience, increase its revenues, and play a major part in rescuing theatre from its present plight.

I write to assist and encourage the prospective builders of tomorrow's American theatres—clients, architects, and consultants. This book is not a prescription for specific design details, but rather an outline for methods and procedures of planning.

In reviewing theatre development through the ages, I do not aim to write an erudite, scholarly history, but a background sketch of the major influences that still govern our theatre shapes today. There are many books to which planners and designers may turn for complete histories. Nor is this book primarily about world theatre, or even European theatre. Even post-World War II, European theatres have been designed for a different economy—one that has complete state or civic subsidy, as well as vastly different labor union pressures. Therefore, though the history of Western European theatre has formed the tradition of our theatre shapes, the theatres I am concerned with are those built in America, today.

Based on my own experiences of forty-four years as a designer of settings, costumes, and lighting, and as a consultant and collaborating designer of theatre shapes, I point out basic faults and omissions in much of current theatre planning. I outline the proper procedures of planning, designing, and building theatres, and offer recommendations on the sensitive but significant role of the theatre consultant. It is my hope to help planners avoid mistakes in future theatres, and to inspire some much needed new thinking about the directions that future theatres should take. With this guide, I hope, clients and architects will be able to avoid the program inadequacies that have caused many theatre projects to be expensive monuments that are unable to meet the needs and expectations of their users.

What Is a Theatre?

All theatre interiors consist of two essential areas: one is "the auditorium," which is designed specifically for the audience; the other, designed for the production, we know as "the stage." These two areas are entirely different, but cannot function fully if unrelated. Independently they have no life; together they produce a living theatre. It is therefore the sensitive interrelationship of the two that makes a theatre design either a success or a failure. All other areas and all external forms must be additive to and enhance these inner functions.

The shapes of these two fundamental areas in a good theatre interior are never accidental. Nor is good theatre design the result of architectural whim or fancy. Rather, the best theatre shapes have been carefully molded by men who were zealous in enhancing the arts of the theatre. They range from acute and sensitive clients to imaginative and professional stage directors, actor-managers, designers, and architects.

In spite of the technical equipment necessary for a theatre, one cannot call its interior either a scientific laboratory (since art is not scientific), nor a pure workshop (since no tangible items are made there), nor a studio (although art forms are created there). Rather it is akin to a dedicated place where people gather to take part in a rite. A theatre planning team must understand this rite before any valid theatres will be designed.

People are drawn to the theatre, not merely to be observers, but essentially to share in a communal experience. When an audience is moved to laughter or tears, we act not only as individuals but as a group. What we have in common is not a creed, not a mutual faith, but kindred emotional and intellectual sympathies. When members of an audience are seated, shoulders almost touching and only slightly separated from the surrounding rows, even the repressed individual infectiously responds to the reactions of his neighbors.

So many times, I have chuckled at an author's lines on first reading the manuscript. Then, in the final run-through, before the arrival of costumes and scenery, I find the lines even more delightful. Although I am only one of three or four people, I laugh openly. A few nights later, as part of an audience, that line causes us all to react with a simultaneous roar of enjoyment. I react to this line in a completely different way because I am now in communication with the rest of the audience.

Without an understanding of this ritualistic experience in the theatre, no good theatre shapes can be formed. It would be equal folly to plan and design a church without knowledge of the basic creed of the congregation, or a detailed understanding of their liturgical customs—or their past traditions.

The Cultural Explosion

Conditions in America force present-day theatre designers to do pioneer work. Theatre arts today are in a state of enormous vitality and constant flux. Since 1955, we have witnessed unprecedented ambition, scope, and action in theatre building. Over four hundred theatres have been constructed.

Nor has energetic building activity been expressed in theatre arts alone. The national desire to enjoy performing arts of all kinds has led to new ballet companies and new symphony orchestras. New museums have been organized, and the desire to collect modern painting and sculpture has become a national pastime. Community leaders have got together and energetically raised enormous sums to build "cultural centers."

Although colleges and universities had been building theatres for some years, they also caught this high fever of the late 1950s and 1960s. Even high schools have planned elaborate theatres that would have been unheard of until recently. Significantly the predominant impetus in theatre design and building has not come from New York, but from other areas of our continent where the stimulation of regional—educational, civic, and community—theatre has been extraordinary.

For the most part almost none of this new theatre building has been commercial. The commercial theatre's primary financial investments are in metropolitan areas and in extensive road touring systems, and they have been strangely inactive during this new building expansion. The commercial theatre has been slow to tear down outmoded and ineffectual theatres, and equally slow to replace them with imaginative, efficient, and attractive new theatre shapes. Basically, the reason has been the traditional absentee landlord's resistance to any significant change in the existing theatre, or to any participation in new approaches for new theatres. Influential corporations, who control theatres in a number of different cities, are naturally reluctant to make radical changes in their investments. Certainly, the building of new theatres would automatically transform their old theatres into less desirable and possibly unrentable buildings; perhaps this is a strong reason for their reluctance to participate in the explosion in theatre construction.

Although I applaud the general aims of our nationwide theatre-building program, far too many of its structures have been hastily put together; too many have been rushed into steel and concrete without the much needed, thoroughly worked out programming that only the future users of those technical structures can provide. This lack of careful, serious, and knowledgeable planning is one of the most serious problems threatening theatre today.

Not all theatre architecture since the mid-1950s has been conceived illegitimately and born in travail, however. There are some outstanding examples of predesign planning and postplanning execution, although they are in the minority. They are proof that only with careful collaboration can good theatre come into being and mature. On the whole, during this cultural explosion, universities have built the better theatres. Interdisciplinary departments (communications, speech, or drama) are staffed by knowledgeable, well-educated people eager to *plan* an efficient and challenging theatre.

The Ford Foundation project of 1962—The Ideal Theatre: 8 Concepts—was a milestone in recent design. Under the direction of W. McNeil Lowry, eight theatre men—mostly stage designers and engineers—were invited to join with eight architects to portray in plans and models their concepts of what today's and tomorrow's theatre should be. Out of it came a widely exhibited group of models and drawings which was also published in book form. The project clearly points out the need for close collaboration between architects and theatre artists. The Ford Foundation has also given generous financial support and encouragement to a number of civic ventures. Among them are the Arena Stage in Washington, D.C., the Tyrone Guthrie Theatre in Minneapolis, Minnesota, and the Alley Theatre in Houston, Texas.

But there is much work to be done. We must educate the various people involved in planning and design of theatres about what the shapes of our theatre actually are and what they might become.

Who Plans Our Theatres?

If the shape of a theatre is to be valid, a team of three people must be involved in the planning and design of new theatre buildings—the owner/client/user, the architect, and the theatre expert. Basically the client governs overall economics. The consultant integrates traditional theatre practice with sometimes inventive developments of that practice. The architect manipulates the sculptural effects of space, building materials, and social amenities.

Throughout history, clients have been those who have financially sponsored the production of plays as well as the building of theatres: the priests (who determined ritual and therefore the shape of a performance area), the state, and wealthy patrons. Later patrons were the speculative investor and the entrepreneur, and primary importance was attached to putting the theatre on a self-supporting basis.

In modern theatre, a client is often a civic body, or government, or private citizen—a foundation executive, a college president, or a regent in the educational theatre. State and municipal committees also guide the creation of community theatres. The client, it seems, is rarely a theatre person—most theatres are built by public-spirited citizens. Naturally, if he has knowledge about theatre arts and the problems facing theatre today, he will be a client who stimulates the best efforts in an architect/designer team; the least effective client is the one who attempts to dominate design ideas without creative awareness or sufficient knowledge of theatre crafts. Often a client is the actual user of the planned theatre. But, if he is not, he must make available to his architect and consultant the advice of the men who will be using the planned theatre.

The first blame in faulty theatre design—and usually the most expensive—must be laid directly at the door of clients. In most cases the working members of the staff of artists, directors, and technicians have not even been brought in to work on the program. It is their mandate as future operators of the theatre that makes the difference between a meaningful program and one that is static and threadbare.

Initially the planning committee must include full representation of its artistic director and his staff of designers and lighting technicians. Only their collaboration with the consultant can determine the final list of primary needs. Unless this is done thoroughly, the first failures will remain to plague the project—maybe the errors will never be corrected.

The skill of an architect in providing an efficacious, economical, and imaginative solution to a problem or need is dependent, like the skill of a medical doctor, on his ability to elicit from a client (even from an unknowledgeable, intractable, or inarticulate client) the true scope and details of the actual problem. He must also elicit a willingness to follow his prescription.

It must be stated emphatically that only the eventual operator of future American theatres can and should spell out the mandate that determines the shape of a theatre interior. It is shocking how many millions are being squandered today under programs dominated by client-donors who give generously to a building program which is in reality a memorial mausoleum. Too much of their donation goes into structure and not a penny into sustaining subsidy.

Financing the Arts

Throughout history, the theatre has been financed by the church, the state, or wealthy patrons. But the young American Republic, renouncing all European political and social establishments, also rejected such forms of cultural subsidy. For our ancestors, patronage was associated with royal domination; state support of the arts was therefore shunned. As our democracy became more prosperous during the nineteenth century, we recognized the need for cultural expression. But the suspicion lingered on that subsidy in the arts was subservience.

Only in recent years have some timid moves in the directions of federal, state, and community backing been made. As a whole, this nation still fails to recognize that the fine arts and performing arts can bloom only under some stable form of subsidy. In this country, local state subsidy would be preferable to federal aid. Federal controls and strictures will interfere with and hinder artistic investigation. The cultural backgrounds and interests of our federal representatives (with a few splendid exceptions) are sadly and embarrassingly not conducive to artistic respect. For the most part, our representatives have not yet gained the cultural understanding and appreciation of the arts that seems to allow French, English, German, Italian, and other European legislators to give wise and unprejudiced support to the arts.

Needless to say, an endorsement of government subsidy is no denunciation of free enterprise in the theatre. In a free-enterprise society there will always be both speculative theatre—sometimes paying its own way quite glamorously—and theatres that must be subsidized institutions. Although limited by having to produce on a profit basis, our commercial theatre has contributed most of the high spots in dramatic achievement since the turn of the century.

After the first World War, in several colleges and communities, ambitious playwrights and directors such as those of the Portmanteau Theatre in California, the Pasadena Playhouse, the Goodman Theatre in Chicago, and New York's Band Box Theatre, the Provincetown Playhouse, and the Theatre Guild all began to struggle toward success. At the same time, a few of Broadway's intelligent producers, such as Arthur Hopkins, produced some of the greatest achievements of the twentieth-century American theatre—the Barrymore *Hamlet,* for example. Later some of the most hard-boiled Broadway commercial managers gave lavish and sensitive support to Eugene O'Neill, Tennessee Williams, Elmer Rice, Clifford Odets, Arthur Miller, Maxwell Anderson, and Philip Barry. Many of these productions were both financial successes and artistic achievements.

Intentionally, I do not distinguish between commercial and subsidized theatre on the basis of their being either professional or amateur. I have no faith in the terms "professional," "amateur," "semi-amateur," and so on. All these are meaningless. Whether an actor is paid or not does not determine his performance. The same is true of the scene designer. The only thing that matters is whether his achievement is good or not. So I would rather make reference to good and bad, creative and noncreative, and stop categorizing when referring to influences and achievement. It is not essential whether an organization must make a great outlay to its members and designers, but rather whether it must take in a profit or not, and where the money must come from. Besides, the increasing number of professional companies in subsidized educational institutions is making that distinction between professional and amateur less clear.

Today, educational and the professional Broadway theatre remain widely separated in their attitudes toward each other, as well as in their operations. An unwillingness to understand persists on both sides. Many Broadway professionals look down their noses at the educational theatre, not recognizing the enormous influence it could have on Broadway. On the other side, many educational theatre people consider their sphere as the *only* artistic, creative, and experimental theatre.

Any theatre production done with originality and freshness, whether with a new manuscript or a reinterpreted classic, deserves to be called experimental. Such originality, freshness, and reinterpretation can occur on Broadway, Off-Broadway, or in regional and educational theatres. One has only to look at the lists of Broadway productions of the last fifty years—the plays, the direction, the performances, the designs—to recognize its highly experimental nature.

Many of these "experimental" productions paid off handsomely, in spite of the high standards that motivated the creative teams, and the financial chances they took. "Experimental," then, should be used to designate what is truly experimental wherever it occurs. Experimentation with new ideas is the aim of any truly professional theatre person no matter where he is working; it is not the exclusive aim of any single area of theatre.

Unfortunately, because of the physical limitation of our commercial theatres, none of these fine productions could survive without full houses. This was a problem European theatres did not have; there an artistic play can survive in repertory because of economic support from a less artistic, but more popular play alternating with it. Since Broadway is the creative hub of touring attractions, it is the center of the professional commercial theatre all over the country—even though there have been recent movements toward decentralization.

Basically, the physical needs—the architectural requirements of theatres, which the client and user must determine—whether Broadway or educational, amateur or professional, are the same except in the matter of size. This problem I will discuss, in detail, later.

What Is the Role of the Architect?

The architect is a professional with a thorough knowledge of his craft, but probably not of the rather specialized field of theatre design. The architect will find himself faced with writing a program for a client who generally does not know exactly what he wants. He must plan a building that will work now and ten years from now, even if the basic purpose of the theatre has changed. The architect will also find that the theatre itself is in the process of growth, change, and experimentation; and that there are no traditional solutions, for the most part, for him to follow. The architect will have to background himself in historical theatre and stage design—who has been designing, who is now designing, and what work is being done. He will probably find that he needs to call in a theatre consultant to keep him informed about all areas of theatre craft.

In the long run, it is the architect who will be responsible for translating the information from all his sources to create a new architectural language for the theatre. It is the architect who will balance the client's concerns, the needs of the professional users, and the special knowledge of the consultant to shape a modern theatre. Matters of theatre exteriors are solely the province of the architect.

What Is the Role of the Consultant?

The function of the theatre consultant is to be a man who provides an overall broad knowledge of the theatre. Ideally, his background might be that of a stage designer, actor-manager, or director. The consultant will be of invaluable assistance to the client/architect team in indicating some of the technical considerations—set designing, lighting, backstage equipment, sightlines, auditorium seating, and facilities for performers. While not being an expert in any one area, the theatre consultant will be aware of "trouble spots" and have access to more specialized assistance in the necessary areas.

It is my belief that only a man steeped in the traditions of the theatre can shape modern theatre effectively. No vital contemporary theatre can be based on tradition alone. But knowledge of all the past solutions by earlier innovators—both the failures and successes—will produce the best designs for today and the future.

II

The Development of the Open-Thrust Stage

Throughout man's history, theatre has persisted as a communal participation in both religious ritual and the pleasure derived from performance. At some periods it has been inspired primarily by a mystical involvement in religious images and ideas. In other ages, it has seemed to focus on the spellbinding performance of verbal, visual, and choreographic talents. In all ages, however, it has expressed a cultural instinct to participate in a communicative involvement.

As a means of mass participation, theatre has, therefore, been affected by the texture of society. When tribes, towns, and cities have practiced a single, all-pervasive religious ritual, theatre audiences have been melded together as a consistent unit. Historically, religious drama has brought entire cities and nations together as a single class—from the highest civic dignitary to the lowliest citizen. The wealthy and the poor alike, in terms of financing also, supported the same religiocivic theatre.

In periods when man was less inspired by religion, however, his cultural urge for such mass communication did not wane. A secular theatre evolved in those times, and it appeared to offer pleasures derived purely from performance. Then the homogeneous audience of the religious theatre became fragmented into a theatre of the aristocracy on the one hand, and a popular theatre on the other. The secular ages showed a division of society into classes. The wealthy aristocracy became patrons of court performances produced exclusively for their peers. The populace flocked to the performances of street players and singers, circuses and spectacles—which were predominantly self-supporting, commercial ventures. Each theatre appealed to the needs—and to the means—of distinct social and intellectual classes.

The shapes of our theatres reflect these changing social structures as well as the patronage that sponsored and built them.

Primitive Drama

Man's desire to communicate with an audience by expressing himself dramatically is as old as the spoken word itself. The most primitive man was a social animal, and one with senses the wild creatures around him did not possess—a divine sense of humor and an extraordinary sense of reasoning. His need to communicate wonder, fear, terror and joy, humor and imagination could not be contained merely in words—nor did a small family unit suffice as an audience.

We can conjecture that a primitive hunter, able to tell a good story, may well have been the first playwright—even the first actor. He may have been, at first, simply the most verbose member of the tribe, the one with the loudest voice, the greatest ability to elaborate and illustrate his story. The more imaginative he was—the greater his talent and the keener his sense of wonder and fear—the more likely he was to elaborate his story.

The storyteller gradually chose the place of his performance, the hour, even the lighting. Sitting around the campfire after a day's hunting, he would put his back to a great boulder. His shadow playing across the boulder would exaggerate his gestures. Fellow tribesmen sitting on sloping ground around him on three sides could see clearly. With a charred piece of wood, he could draw on the rock behind him a crude but expressive outline of the mastodon he had killed—or perhaps the mastodon that got away.

Here were all the basic elements of theatre: a story with a climax, verbal embellishment, a seating arrangement, lighting, and scenery. Here also was the first Open-Thrust Stage—one that is surrounded by the audience on three sides.

The Birthplace of Theatre

From the primitive Greek celebrations of Dionysiac rites gradually developed the glory and art of theatre. Every early civilization had some form of ritual, such as the Egyptian Alydos Passion Play or the Osiris myth, that might have developed into theatre, but in Western civilization, only the Greeks developed a theatrical art form independent of its religious background.

It was the site of the Greek outdoor religious rituals that became the earliest formal theatre, while their liturgical format influenced the shape of the theatre. At the Dionysiac rites, which started in predawn light, choral dancers naturally formed a circle around the altar stone. This became the circular orchestra or chorus area of Greek theatre. Around the orchestra—the first architecturally formulated Open-Thrust Stage—the audience sat in a semicircle on three sides.

In his history, Herodotus describes the primitive theatres of his day. Situated on steep hillsides, the seating and steps were cut into the terrain and secured by wooden planks and braces. A single-story wood structure was set behind the chorus area.

Eventually Greek theatres—the seats, the flat round orchestra, and the *skene* backing up the chorus area (from which we derive our word "scene")—were all built of stone. Built into the *skene* were three formal entrances facing the audience. Wing structures, called *periaktoi,* were added right and left to create a formal three-sided setting.

The stark simplicity of this early theatre gradually gave way to more elaborate stagecraft and production. Painted scenery was introduced. A manually operated winch was used to lower figures of the gods from the top of the *skene.* Set-changing devices were employed, like wheeled wagons and three-sided pylons that could be rotated to expose different set images. More and more elaborate devices were introduced until visual embellishments and physical paraphernalia shared attention equally with the spoken word. Yet, for stage lighting, the Greeks wisely, if of necessity, relied on the ultimate visual drama of the developing sunrise.

As theatre architecture developed, so did the drama itself. Formalized storytelling and formalized acting, chanting, and dancing ultimately blossomed into the great period of Greek theatre. Aeschylus, Sophocles, Euripides, and Aristophanes created a dramatic art so rich that it has influenced theatre ever since.

Roman Elaborations

Like so much of their culture, the theatre of the Romans was completely inspired by the Greeks. However, in taking over the Greek theatre shape, the Romans made several significant changes.

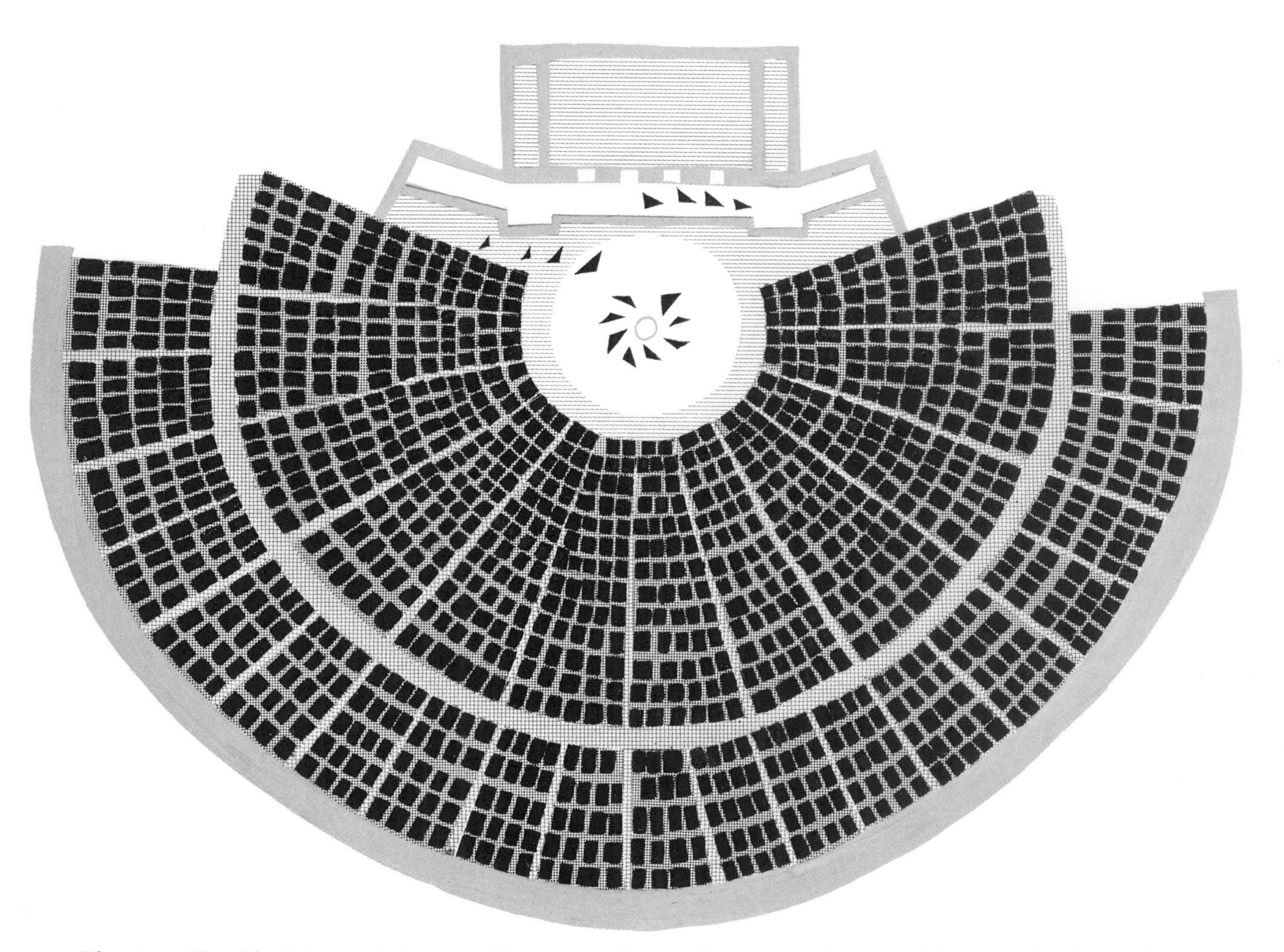

Fig. 1. The birthplace of theatre: The Open-Thrust Stage was developed by the Greeks in the fourth and fifth centuries B.C. to get the greatest number of people as close as possible to the performing area.

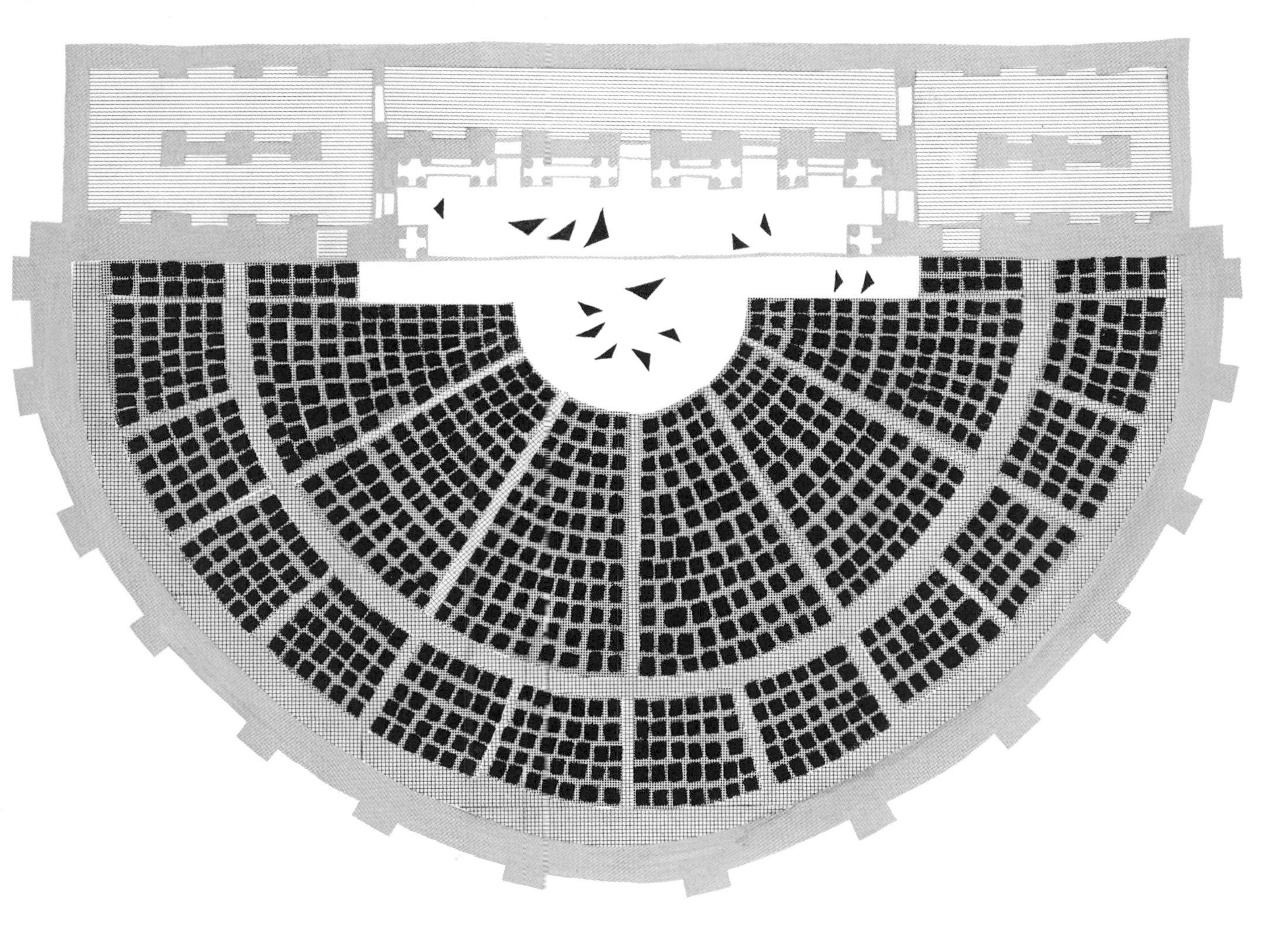

Fig. 2. The Romans elaborated the basic Greek theatre shape from the first century B.C. through the fourth century A.D.

Since the chorus had become a fairly stationary speaking body, the circular orchestra, no longer used for dances, was reduced to a semicircle. The remaining space provided seats of honor for dignitaries. Although the Roman stage was still open in the sense that it was in the same room with the audience, its thrust into the audience area, and the extent of audience seating surrounding it on three sides were markedly reduced.

The stage itself became a raised platform, ensuring an unobstructed view for everyone. Behind the stage, the *skene* became more formal and elaborate, in some cases reaching a height of three or four stories. Often the stage was roofed and a canopied sunshade stretched over the audience—thereby integrating stage and audience into one tight architectural unit.

Abandoning the surrounding hillsides, the Romans began to situate their theatres on flat land, often inside their towns. Here, no longer relying on the terrain for slope, they constructed steeply raked seating of masonry.

Roman stagecraft went even beyond the Greeks in developing technical equipment. Enormous arenas, such as the Colosseum in Rome, housed spectacles of unmatched elaborateness: large-scale pyrotechnics, chariot races, wild animal acts, and even the fabled naval battles in flooded arenas.

Terence and Seneca, Andronicus, Naevius, and the much applauded Plautus, writing either to be read or performed, gave Roman theatre a completely secular character. And as they developed elaborate spectacles, more human, political, and social satires, Roman theatre broke away entirely from all associations with religious ritual.

The Mysteries and the Passion Plays

In the late fifth and sixth centuries, with Rome in decline and ecclesiastical power increasing, the theatre found itself without stage patronage and condemned by Christian authorities. Permanent theatre, as such, disappeared; nevertheless, strolling players, acrobats, jugglers, puppeteers, and ballad singers in the streets attracted crowds throughout Western Europe.

It was by a strange quirk that dramatic art again found a new home within the very church that had banished it to the marketplace and street corner. Just as the church fostered stained-glass windows and illuminated manuscripts as a vital means of interpreting the Bible for an illiterate flock, so the church also turned to dramatic art to enliven ecclesiastical ritual.

Around the ninth century, religious plays developed within the liturgy of the mass. At Eastertide, the antiphonal responses between the three Marys and the angel at the sepulcher (beginning "*Quem quaeritis*"—"Whom seek ye?") were the genesis of a play about the divine mystery of the Passion. Other plays depicting the miraculous lives of the saints also developed.

These mystery and miracle plays were first performed on the steps of the altar or the chancel. This setting was essentially a platform Open Stage, with virtually no thrust (except possibly into the choir) since the performance was viewed primarily from the front.

As the productions became extremely popular, attracting much larger audiences, the plays themselves became increasingly secular. In an effort to accommodate large audiences and to separate the religious from the secular, the clergy moved the productions to the broad steps outside the church. Here, the Open Stage arrangement with minimal thrust remained virtually the same.

With potential audience space more than quadrupled, the plays gave less emphasis to religious ceremony and sermonizing and more to attracting and entertaining audiences. Supplementary actors were enlisted, principally from the laymen in the trade guilds. As the clergy withdrew, the guilds took over the productions and their financing entirely. Lay actors ad-libbing introduced vernacular into the plays until eventually the Latin in which they were originally performed was entirely replaced by the vernacular.

This secularization encouraged more elaborate staging techniques: water, fire, and gunpowder brought to physical life the church's spiritual "fire and brimstone." Later, wheeled platform stages were drawn around the marketplace and through the town like the floats in contemporary parades. The ancestors of modern mobile theatres, they permitted actors to play to standing audiences and to spectators on surrounding balconies. The platform stages permitted viewing from three sides, reintroducing the three-sided Open-Thrust Stage shape.

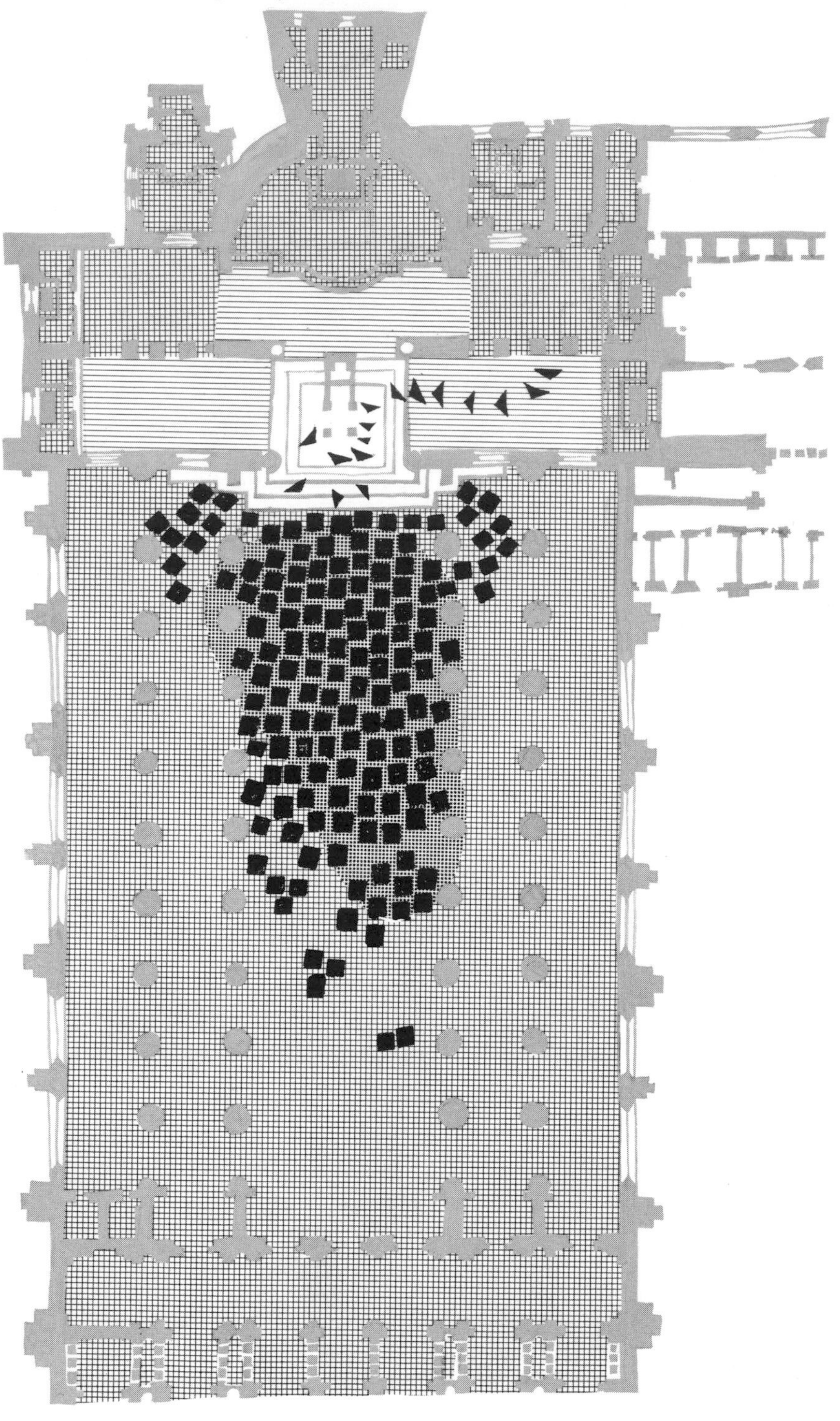

Fig. 3. In the Middle Ages, mystery and passion plays were performed before the church altar.

Fig. 4. To accommodate larger audiences, the church moved the mystery and passion plays outdoors onto the steps of the cathedral.

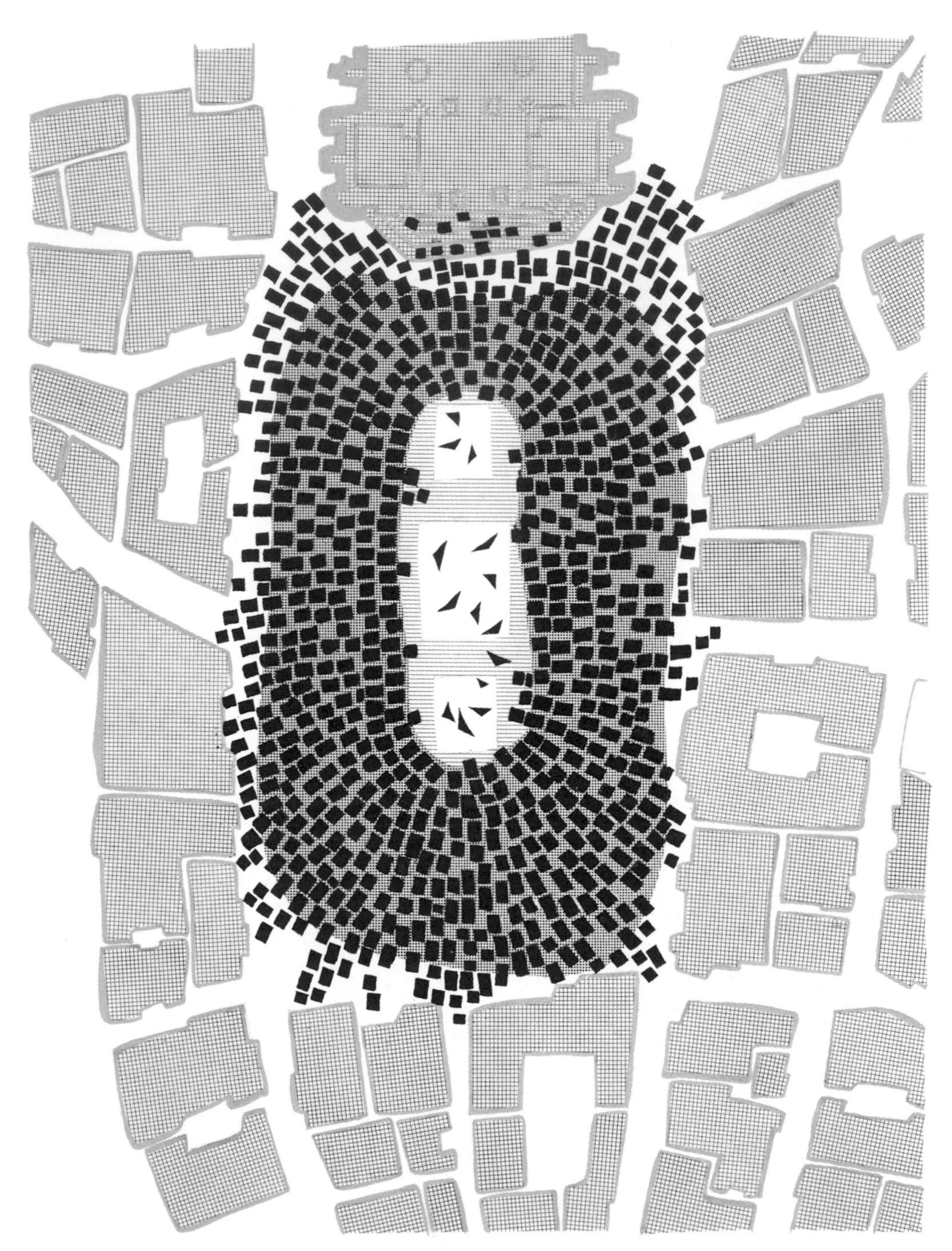

Fig. 5. As medieval secular theatre became popular, three-sided wagon stages were set up in the marketplaces.

Renaissance of the Greco-Roman Shape

The fifteenth-century Renaissance in Italy brought a renewed interest in all the arts—especially those of ancient Greece. Ruling princes and popes, the patrons of this artistic revival, turned neither to the cathedral steps nor to the marketplaces for their theatre spaces. Instead, they attempted to re-create the Greek architectural forms of twenty centuries earlier.

The Teatro Olimpico at Vicenza, started by Palladio in 1580 and finished in 1584 by Scamozzi, shows how the Greco-Roman designs were taken over and adapted. The semicircular seating plan of Greco-Roman theatre became a semiellipse, anticipating the change of the classical orchestra from a performing area to an audience area. Like Roman theatres with roofed stages and canopied seating, the Teatro Olimpico was still a semiexterior plan.

The aristocracy, involved in masques and spectacles that revived the ancient world, based their theatres on private knowledge and scholarly research. It was withdrawn and dissociated from the mainstream of popular theatre. Quite apart, the populace still had a theatre of their own—a survival of the tradition of jugglers and acrobats.

Comedies were produced in the marketplace and staged on elaborate open platform wagons that continued the tradition of medieval wagon stages. The skills of buffoons and clowns, tumblers and magicians were handed down from father to son. They used largely unrecorded material to build traditions of characters, costumes, and properties. These productions, known in Italy as *commedia dell'arte* were self-supporting, speculative, commercial ventures. They had no patronage or financial support from princes of state or church. This was the popular theatre supported by the people.

Strolling Players in the Inn Courtyards

During this period the Open-Thrust Stage continued to develop throughout Europe. In England and Spain, for example, strolling players performed for the populace in the courtyards of

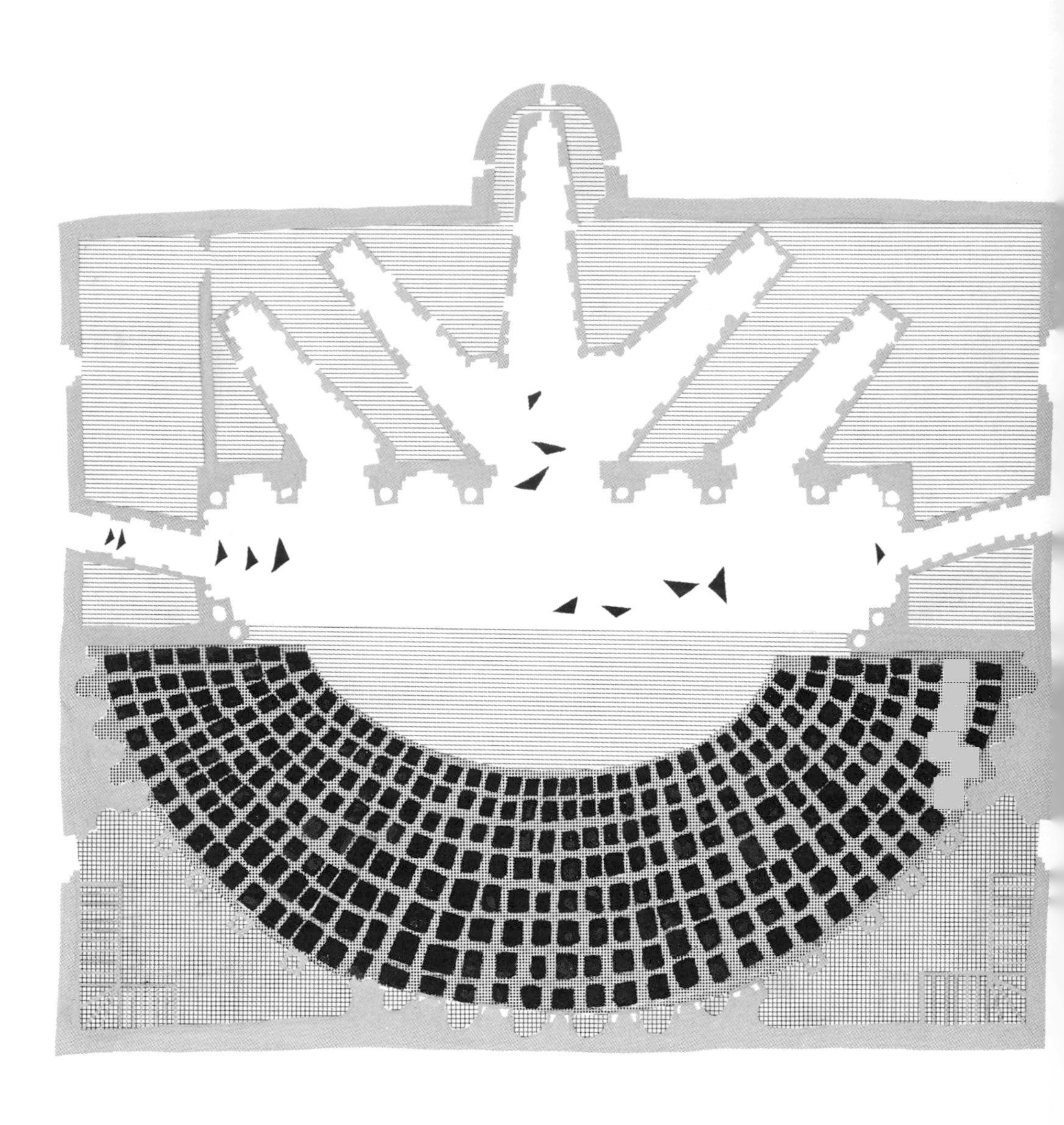

Fig. 6. The Italian Renaissance brought a revival of the Greco-Roman shape, as in the Teatro Olimpico at Vicenza, 1580–1584.

inns, carrying on the tradition of the popularized street theatre.

Temporary stages were set up at one end of the open-air courtyards. The flat ground in the center served as standing room for holders of low-price tickets. Multitiered balconies surrounded the Open Stage on three sides, creating an atmosphere of intimacy and immediacy. Here sat the buyers of more expensive tickets. It was a realization of the Spanish playwright Lope da Vega's basic needs for creating theatre: "Give me four trestles, four boards, two actors and a passion."

Elizabethan Playhouses

A legal injunction against actors performing in the City of London innyards in 1576 prompted actor-manager James Burbage to build outside the city limits the first structure in England devoted entirely to the presentation of plays. Burbage's building, called simply The Theatre, incorporated all the best elements of the inn courtyards into a formal design that became the basis for all Elizabethan playhouses.

Elizabethan stages were Open-Thrust platforms placed at one end of a circular or octagonal court. Behind the stage were two levels of roofed, performing areas, which could be curtained off from the audience and used as entrances and exits and as the settings of small-scale interior scenes.

Like the balconied courtyards of the inns, Elizabethan playhouses had several tiers of galleries around the circular court, providing covered seats for spectators willing to pay more for tickets. In the open space surrounding the stage, other theatregoers sat on benches or stood in what the English call the Pit (because of its similarity to the bear-baiting and cock-fighting pits that had also been used as temporary theatres).

Private theatres were later constructed along the same lines, but with the addition of a roof to cover the entire audience. Little scenery was used. A curtain or two, a few banners and props, and sometimes lavish costumes provided all the visual trappings. Poet-playwrights relied on their verbal imagery to conjure up subliminal pictures. In the Elizabethan theatre, truly, the play was the thing whereby the acting company caught the attention of their audiences. Shakespeare, Marlowe, Ben Jonson, John Webster, Beaumont and Fletcher all wrote for theatres designed to

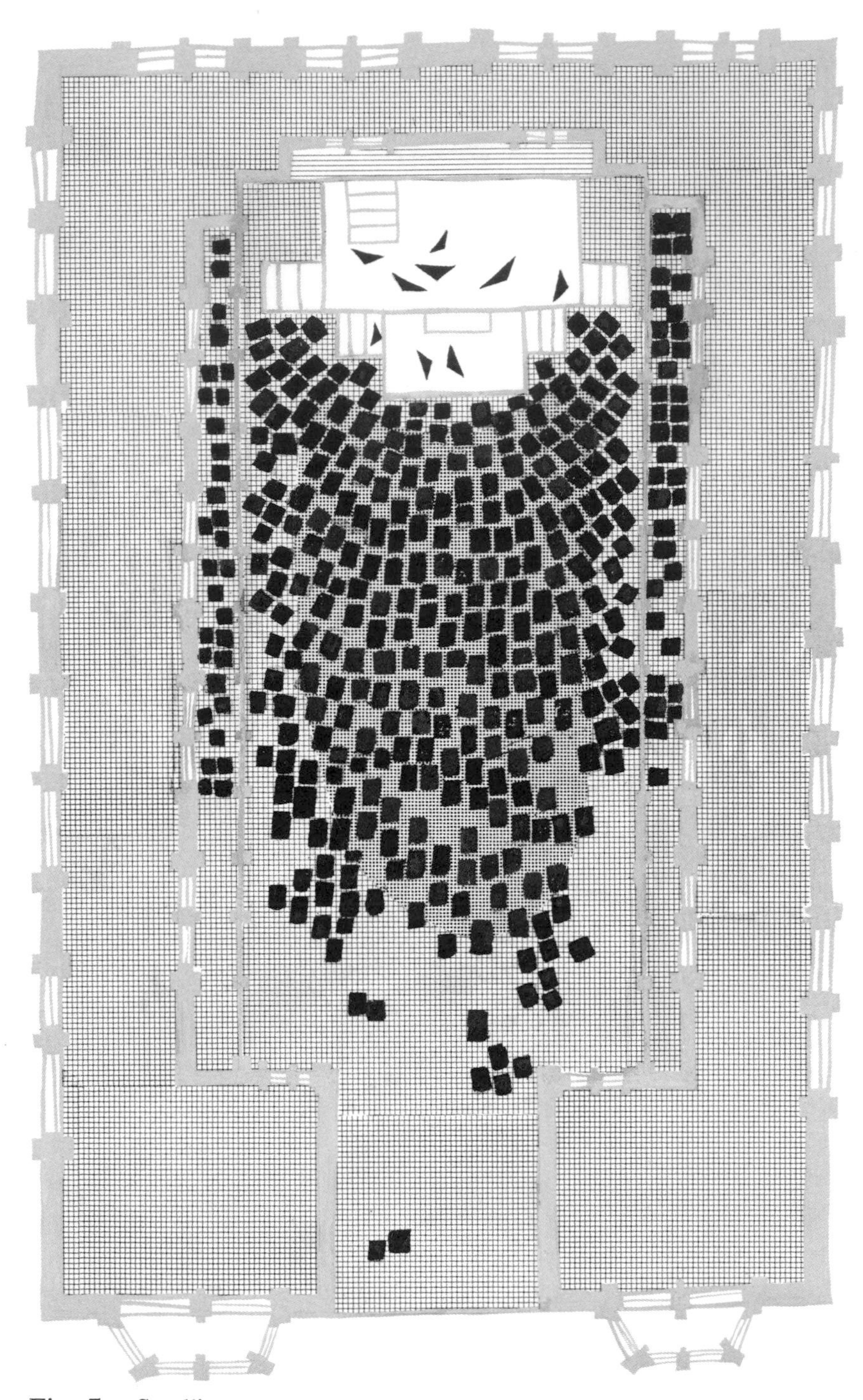

Fig. 7. Strolling players set up temporary Open-Thrust Stages in the courtyards of inns during the fifteenth and sixteenth centuries.

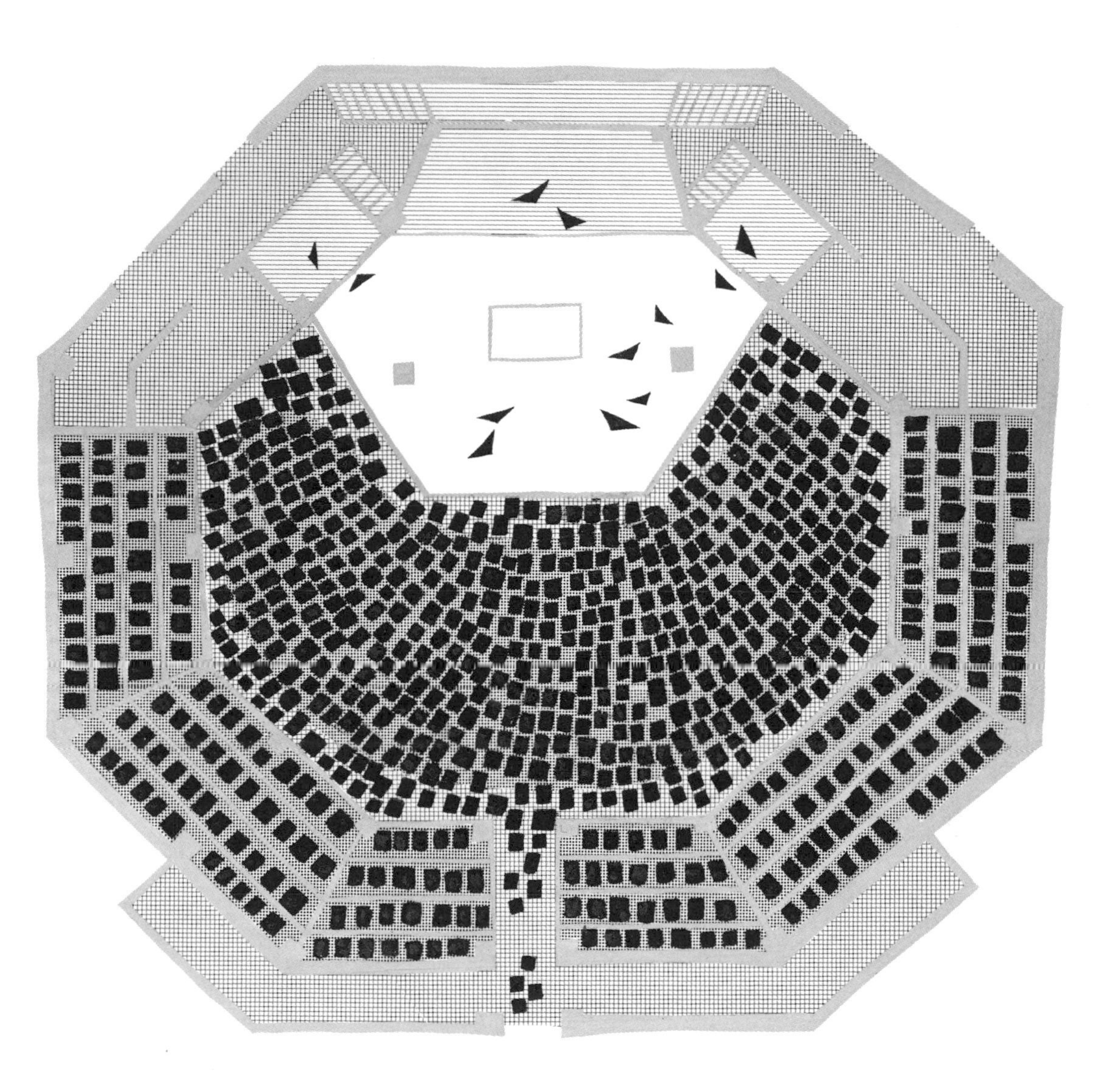

Fig. 8. By the seventeenth century, the Open-Thrust Stage of the courtyards had crystallized into a fixed architectural expression.

focus on the spoken word with an intimacy never previously achieved.

At the end of the sixteenth century in Italy, opera and ballet began to develop. Both these art forms were performed indoors in palace ballrooms and in formal outdoor gardens. Large casts enacted masques, which were a mixture of dance, singing, and procession in great palace halls. The size of these productions, combined with the renaissance of mechanical equipment which was put at the service of elaborating stagecraft, ultimately gave impetus to the development of an entirely new kind of stage. Around 1600 these new Italian concepts of theatre design began to be felt in England and throughout the Western world. So strong was their effect that henceforth they molded the design of theatre stages and auditoriums. Not for three hundred years was the Open-Thrust Stage to be used again.

Fig. 9. Princely patrons organized operas, ballets, and masques in palace ballrooms during the sixteenth and seventeenth centuries.

The Development of the Proscenium Stage

In each age, stagecraft has developed from simple suggestion to technical elaboration. The starkness of early Greek staging gradually gave way to a literal, visual depiction of such symbols as the *deus ex machina* by mechanically lowering the figure of a god from the top of the *skene*. The spectacles of later Rome surpassed those of also every other period, while the late medieval passion and miracle plays spoke literally with fire and brimstone.

This development of increasingly elaborate stagecraft in each age parallels the gradual secularization of theatre from its religious beginnings. As theatrical productions become more secular in their content, stagecraft becomes more detailed in its physical representation of action and the spoken word. It is a development that moves the theatre away from its initial basis in symbolism and suggestion toward an emphasis on the artificial aspects of physical detail.

Another aspect of this increasing detachment or dissociation of theatre from its origins is the gradual enclosure of theatre space —from the outdoor theatres of Greece to the canvas-roofed arenas of later Rome.

In modern theatre also, stagecraft shows a similar development. From the days of our early poet-playwrights, when most attention was paid to the spoken word, theatre has, until recently, shown an increasing concentration on its visual embellishment, on scenic effects and the supporting mechanics of stagecraft. Modern theatre has also succeeded in completely enclosing the auditorium —cutting out all daylight, air, and weather—detaching it from our natural, earthly environment. The effects of these abstractions on the basic function and impact of theatre have been largely ignored.

The Renaissance brought the first new dimension to modern theatre—the visual arts of easel painting, which added a new visual vocabulary to the literature of the theatre. The flowering of architecture, painting, and sculpture in the Renaissance also saw the launching of the first specialized theatre costume designers and the first recorded stage designers. Painted backdrops displaying the rediscovered techniques of perspective came to play an integral part in Western theatre. The elaboration of production techniques was a natural consequence. Flying scenery, trompe l'œil, and mechanical effects were to become as important as actors and musicians. Theatre technicians—architects, designers, actor-managers, builders—virtually became the stars of the era.

Genesis of the Proscenium Frame

The renaissance of the Greco-Roman Open-Thrust Stage also brought adaptations to its *skene*—the building that served as the stage backdrop. The Teatro Olimpico (1580–1584) developed the *skene* further. Three entrances in the back wall, coupled with side entrances through enclosing architecture, produced a three-sided background onstage. The building extended behind each of the five stage entrances, which showed, in perspective, not painted backdrops, but permanently constructed buildings and vistas. Perspective was employed, but it was architectural, not yet actual easel painting. While popular, this effect soon became frustrating to Renaissance artists and stage designers.

The next development of permanent stage vistas came at Sabbionetta, where Scamozzi, in 1588, boldly combined the three arched entrances in the backstage wall into a single large arch. Anxious to exercise their visual talents, artists recognized that this single opening could be used for a single large painting. It was the beginning of the painted backdrop as we know it now. They also saw that it was possible to change these canvases and thereby vastly increase the variety of the visual experience.

It was in the Farnese Theatre at Parma that the true Proscenium theatre was born. Designed by Aleotti in 1618, this 350-seat theatre brought together the separate elements of a single arched opening onto the stage, a curtained stage, a backstage for scenic canvases, and a new seating arrangement. They combined to form the Proscenium theatre. Because of its single arch, the

Fig. 10. The Italian Renaissance also brought the revived art of perspective—seen through a single large arch—to the theatre, as at Sabbionetta in 1588.

Fig. 11. The first true Proscenium theatre was the Teatro Farnese at Parma, 1618.

Proscenium theatre, in effect, houses the audience and the actors in different rooms. There is a stage house on one side of the arch, and the audience watches it from the auditorium room on the other side. The wide, yet shallow, semiellipse plan of earlier auditoriums gave way once the three-arch classical stage was eliminated. The auditorium became not much wider than the Proscenium arch itself. When the semielliptical seating plan of the Teatro Olimpico was narrowed to fit the new theatre at Parma, the effect was to create an auditorium plan that had an arc as the rear wall; continuing into long straight extensions of that arc were side walls.

Proscenium Stagecraft

Naturally, production and staging techniques developed to extend the potential of successively changing painted backdrops. From the late fifteenth century through the seventeenth century a period of great creative development in stage machinery occurred. All the ingenuity of Renaissance engineering worked to develop scene-changing devices and scenic effects. Princes and patrons vied with each other to present for their guests the most elaborate visual extravaganzas. Masters of the craft were in demand in Italy and throughout the Continent. Raphael, Mantegna, and Leonardo designed painted backdrops and flats; Leonardo also made sketches for turntables.

During the height of the baroque age, the talented Italian Galli family, known as the Bibienas, contributed three generations of skillful, imaginative scenic artists. They spent their entire lives developing effects to create an illusion of depth by stressing perspective—an illusion which is still a dominant trend today.

In England, too, this direction seized the imagination of designers such as Inigo Jones, whose technical inquisitiveness and invention dominated the first half of the seventeenth century. Jones carried the Italian Proscenium tradition forward to create a forestage that greatly enhanced productions of court masques by such poets as John Milton. Starting his career with portable platforms and scenery set in rooms at court and in university halls, he soon designed actual theatre buildings. Inigo Jones, was, in fact, the first all-around artist in the theatre. His developments include raked stages, the use of translucent scenery with rear lighting, and moving light changes to heighten the drama. Scene designer, theatre engineer, and architect, he was an inspirational leader for the theatre of his time.

In the eighteenth century, the later Bibienas, the imaginative Juvarra, and Piranese designed opera stage settings that were rich and elaborate. Always an art of romantic opulence, baroque and rococo opera along with ballet were the major influences in courtly theatre architecture during the seventeenth and eighteenth centuries.

These developing stage techniques had a marked influence on the size and shape of theatre buildings. The proportions of the stage itself changed as exaggerated perspective effects became the vogue; by the middle of the seventeenth century, while many theatres had Proscenium openings of about thirty-two feet, the stages were as deep as 132 feet.

Flying scenery also influenced the shape of theatres. And offstage areas had to be extended. When scenery had to be changed rapidly, wings were pulled off in a horizontal plane, to Stage Right and Stage Left; backdrops were raised up into the fly loft or occasionally sunk through slots in the floor. Tall stage lofts had to be built to raise or "fly" these backdrops, which were sometimes thirty or forty feet high. Counterweighted grids to fly the scenery and stage houses to support and enclose them sometimes rose eighty to one hundred feet over the stage floor. All this machinery has had a marked influence on the designing of theatre buildings from that time to the present.

Artificial lighting in the early roofed theatres, such as the semi-enclosed Teatro Olimpico, similarly had an effect on the height of the stage house. Enormous candelabras were set on the stage and in the auditorium, both to decorate and to light the theatre. To provide more air space around the candelabras, thus offsetting the heat and danger of fire, stage sets became deeper and higher. To increase illumination of the stage, primitive footlights were developed: multiple sets of candles were set along the forestage behind a masking, and colored glass was sometimes placed over them to create a moonlight effect.

Focus on Seating Plans

The development of the Proscenium arch and stage house naturally influenced the shape of the audience seating arrange-

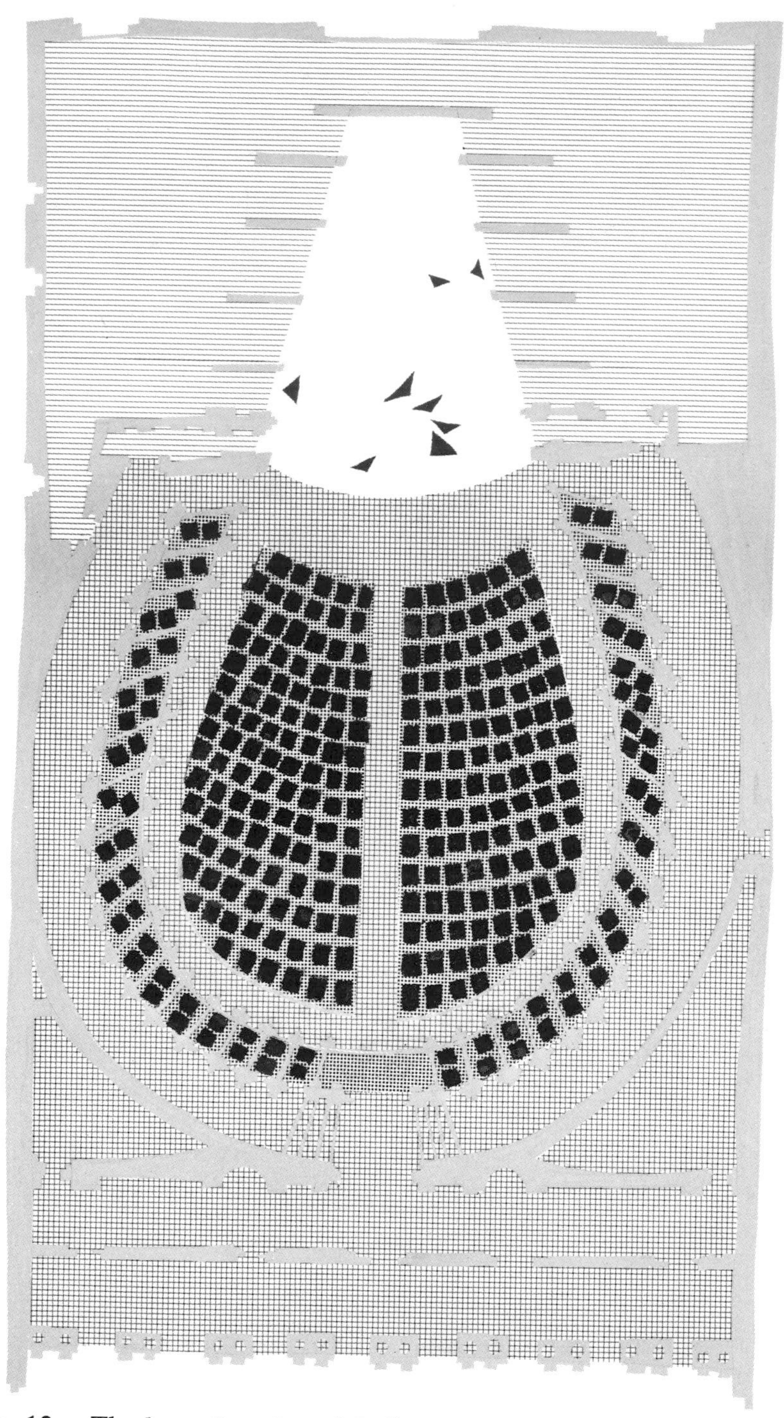

Fig. 12. The horseshoe-shaped Italian theatre developed from the informal arrangement of productions in palace ballrooms.

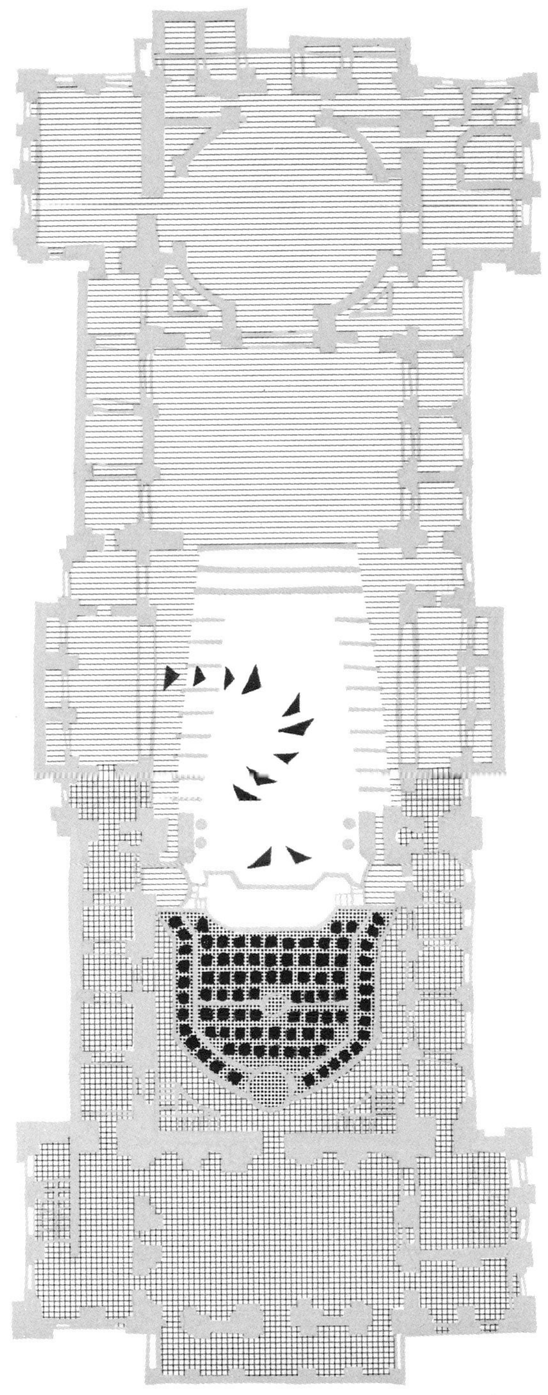

Fig. 13. In the eighteenth century, the deep stage shape reflected the vogue for exaggerated perspective effects.

ments also. As Renaissance one-point perspective became a dominant element in scenic design, the questions of who in the audience was to enjoy the best view became a critical factor in shaping the auditorium. Perspective paintings, designed as if seen from a single point, were obviously best viewed from the center of the house and at a moderate elevation above stage level. It was the patron and his entourage who were given the seats in this location.

In theatres after the Farnese at Parma, the side walls were gradually narrowed to meet a smaller Proscenium opening so that sight lines could be improved. The horseshoe-shaped auditorium that developed came to be known among the English-speaking people as the "Italian Theatre" because it departed so markedly from the English Open-Thrust Stage tradition. This shape, which we now refer to as the Proscenium theatre, was to become so popular that for three centuries only variations and refinements of it would be constructed.

In the early horseshoe auditoriums the princely patron sat front and center in an elevated royal box; his courtiers were arranged in a semicircle of small elevated boxes to his right and to his left. A much larger audience was provided for, not only in the pit—the area which we now call the orchestra—but also in tiers of boxes and galleries above the level of the royal box.

In actuality, the horseshoe seating plan that was developed to accommodate the one-point perspective restated the hierarchical arrangement of stages in outdoor palace gardens and court ballrooms. There the actors played on the same level as the royal patron, his court, and guests. As in Greek theatres, the front part of the orchestra was left free of seats to accommodate courtly dances. At the back of the hall, in the center, sat the duke and his duchess; courtiers and guests sat or stood to the right and left according to their rank.

In the horseshoe theatre, the boxes were primarily angled for enjoyment of a performance; but deference to and vision of the royal patron was a strong element in the design. The audience, taking their cue for approval from the prince, divided their attention between him and the performance. This looking for a cue of approval from someone other than themselves is not a trait limited to Renaissance and baroque audiences. Even today, our theatre public looks to critics for guidance or approval. Fortunately for the shape of contemporary theatres, this look is directed at the pages of a morning newspaper, rather than at a patron in the center of an auditorium.

Theatre architects matched the baroque and rococo opulence of scene designers. Elaborate Proscenium arches, carved and gilded auditoriums with multitiered, shallow balconies and vast foyers and lobbies were the pattern of the age.

In the English theatre, where the emphasis on intimacy of performer and audience lingered, where emphasis remained on the spoken word rather than focusing on the visual production as in Italy, the apron or forestage also survived longer. It created an intimacy that the horseshoe auditorium never could. But after Puritan censorship closed the English theatres for an eighteen-year period (1642–1660), the Restoration monarchy revived and supported theatre, and the horseshoe auditorium became inevitable in England also.

New theatres were built in existing structures, such as the Hampton Court Palace indoor tennis court, where the ground was dug out to give the new stage sufficient height. This lowering of the floor level reemphasized the English designation of the orchestra as "the pit."

The great acting in England at this period helped to preserve the forestage and therefore the intimate scale of the English stage. The best English architects joined forces with producer-managers Sir William Davenant and Thomas Killigrew to design new playhouses reflecting the social and creative atmosphere of their day.

Even though they enjoyed royal patronage, their plans for the first Drury Lane Theatre envisioned a theatre audience composed of both the middle- and upper-middle-class as well as court circles. This was the first public playhouse in England with a royal box, and Charles II, the patron, was the first British monarch to attend a public theatre. His English predecessors had always had the theatre brought to their courts and palaces. This social development showed that it was neither a court theatre, in the continental sense, nor a place for rough entertainment of the masses.

Early studies by the great English architect Christopher Wren for the rebuilding of Drury Lane clearly show a comparatively shallow oval auditorium, wider than it was deep. The raked stage, which was nowhere as deep as continental stages, had a raked apron, with two permanent stage entrances on either side. Above each of the four entrances were boxes for the public. The raked

FIG. 14

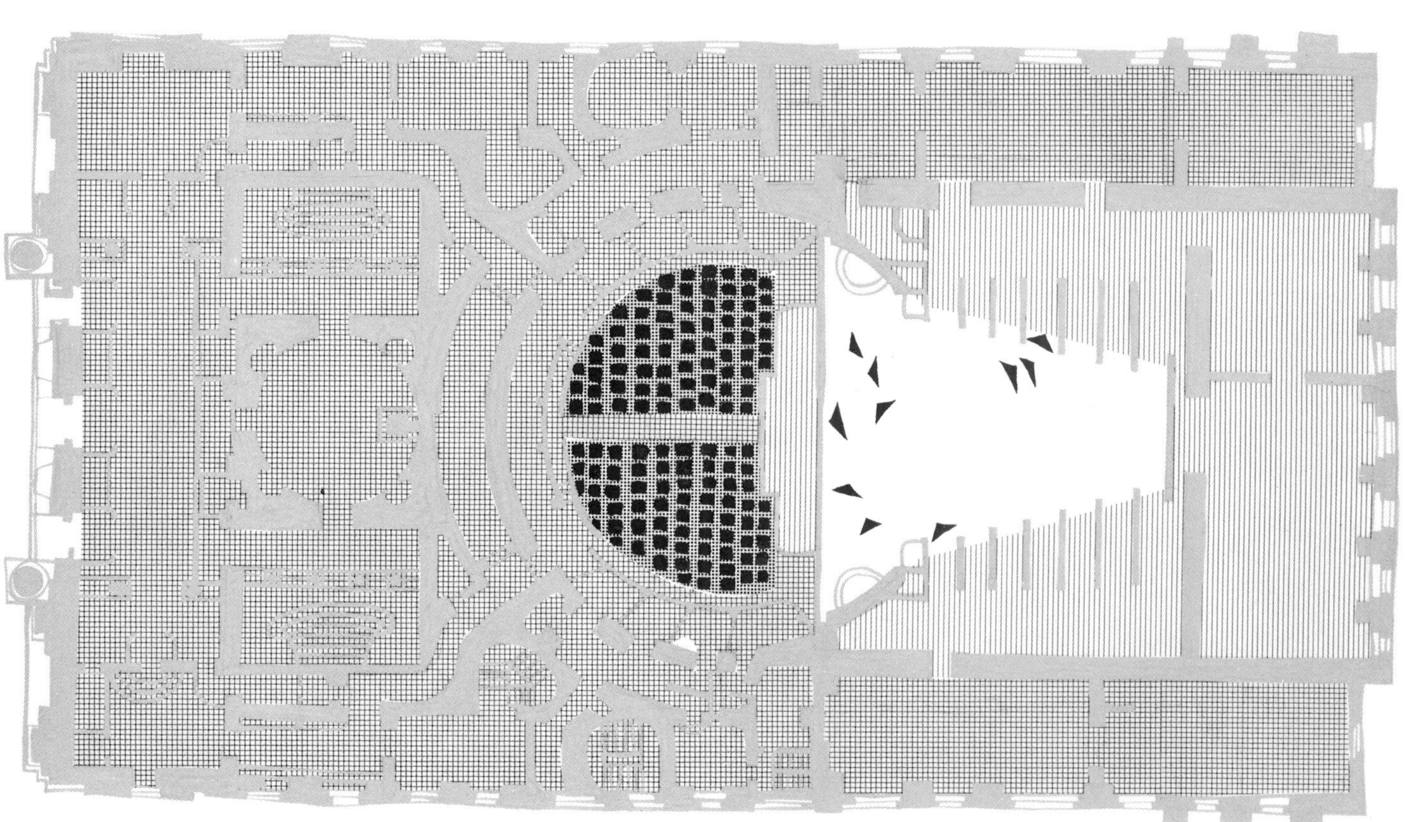

FIG. 15

Figs. 14, 15. Christopher Wren's design for the Drury Lane Theatre shows raked orchestra seating, as well as a raked stage (Fig. 15) which originated with the sixteenth-century techniques of theatrical perspective. An extended forestage with boxes on each side shows the vestiges of the Open Stage tradition (Fig. 14).

pit had benches terminating in the back, on a line slightly below that of the center tier box. This design shows a trend toward an entirely new shape in English theatre.

In eighteenth-century England, however, the increasing popularity of imported Italian opera not only brought about the overthrow of Handelian opera but led to the dominance of the Italian horseshoe auditorium.

Democratic Seating Concept

During the eighteenth century, as the colonies in America grew, theatres were built in Williamsburg in 1712, Philadelphia, Baltimore, and New York in 1749, and in the 1750s many more were being constructed throughout the East. Naturally, they all reflected close cultural ties with the mother countries and, while on a smaller scale, were identical to European theatre plans.

However, the prosperous middle class that grew in size and influence during the late eighteenth and early nineteenth centuries in Europe, as well as in the new states in America, also supported the theatre enthusiastically. Even though financial responsibility was still with wealthy patrons, new theatres began to reflect this middle-class interest and attendance. While the shape of the auditorium remained the same, it grew in size to accommodate numbers of affluent theatregoers. Theatre designs stressed less the formal and conspicuous display of princely patrons and visiting royalty, becoming, instead, more democratic in seating plan.

In the early nineteenth century, theatre boxes were still built right and left of the stage, at the front of the house, but, even these vestiges of three-sided viewing faded as Italian opera gained precedence. All seating became clearly one-sided, facing the Proscenium arch directly; in effect, the auditorium was a separate room from the stage house. In deference to larger audiences, lobbies also became more spacious, and Green Rooms, where the audience could call on performers, were introduced.

Realism and the Box Set

During the nineteenth century, the work of playwrights, stage directors, and stage designers was marked by a reaction to the excessive elaborateness that dominated the preceding hundred years. In its place, during the 1860s, came the realism of Ibsen.

Although dramatists do not, as a rule, directly prescribe changes in the shape of theatres, to meet and complement Ibsen's literary realism, stage directors and designers discarded the old, elaborate romantic settings. The new realism in design led to the development of the "box set," a minutely realistic room, the fourth wall of which is missing to allow the audience to view the action.

Realistic sets were heavier and more solid in design and construction, and as a consequence, backstage storage space and actual stage area had to be increased. In addition, realistic sets demanded the elimination of artificial viewing angles. The movement toward good sight lines with equal viewing opportunity for the entire audience began with Gottfried Semper's design, which Richard Wagner used for his opera house built in Bayreuth, Germany, in 1876. The auditorium was fan-shaped, with a steeply raked orchestra floor. Only two shallow balconies bridged the rear wall. In Bayreuth was the first installation of "Continental seating," a plan that eliminates traditional aisles on the orchestra level, and increases the spaces between rows so that they serve as aisles. At Bayreuth, to the right and left of these aisle rows was a separate foyer outside the auditorium.

While the pitched floor provided a clear view over the heads in front—thereby increasing the sense of visual and aural intimacy between audience and performers—the seats were laid out in straight lines. Unknown to Bayreuth's designers, the year before, two Frenchmen, Davioud and Bourdais, had worked out an adroitly curved seating plan that staggered the seats one behind the other to provide even better sight lines. Their theatre was never executed but their "dish" design is now considered essential in solving the sight lines of fan-shaped auditoriums.

The stage at Bayreuth had the most modern machinery for moving scenery. And for the first time, an orchestra pit was almost completely concealed by lowering it between the stage and the audience. Part of its area was actually under the stage, with a rear wall that acted as an acoustical shell deflecting the music out into the audience, and with part of it also under the first few rows of orchestra seats.

Bayreuth's greatest single contribution by far was the auditorium seating design. Despite the straight-line seating, it is still accepted as the best early solution to the problems of sight lines.

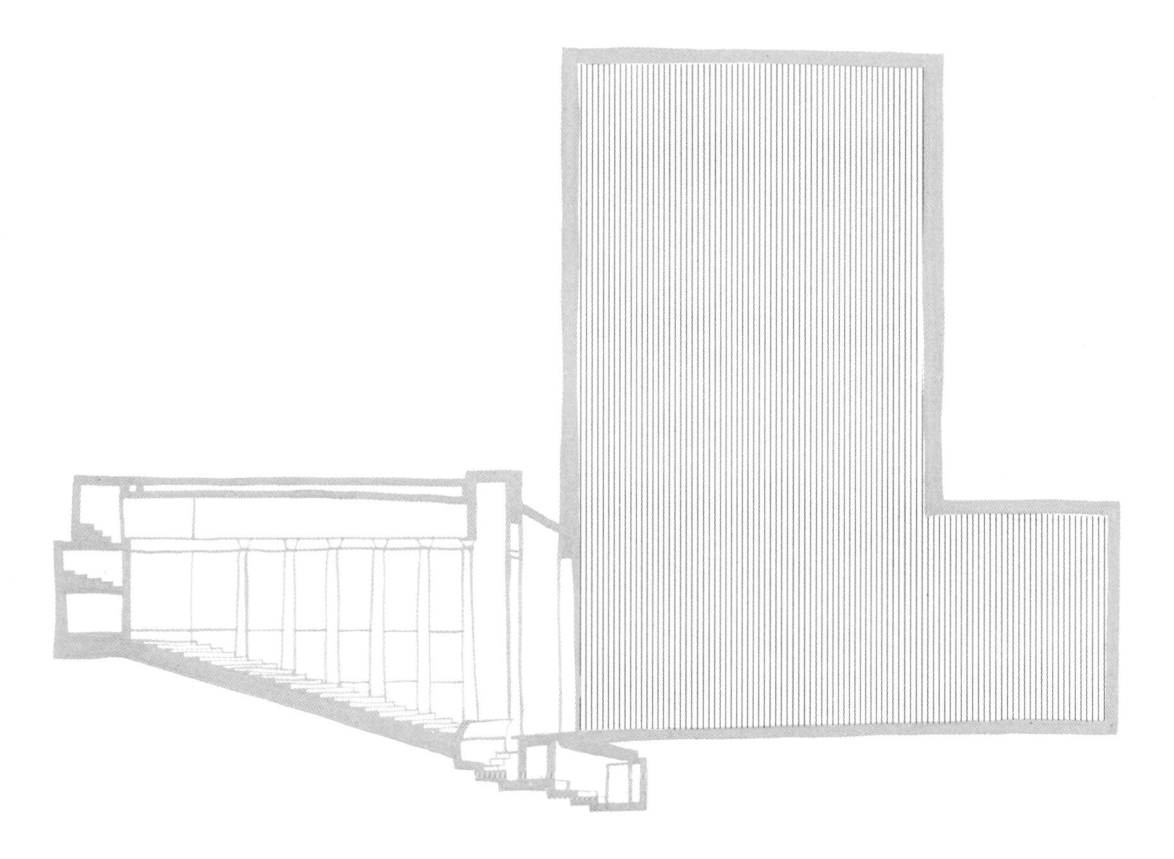

Figs. 16, 17. The shape of Richard Wagner's Opera House in Bayreuth, Germany, 1876, is a model for continental seating and stage machinery.

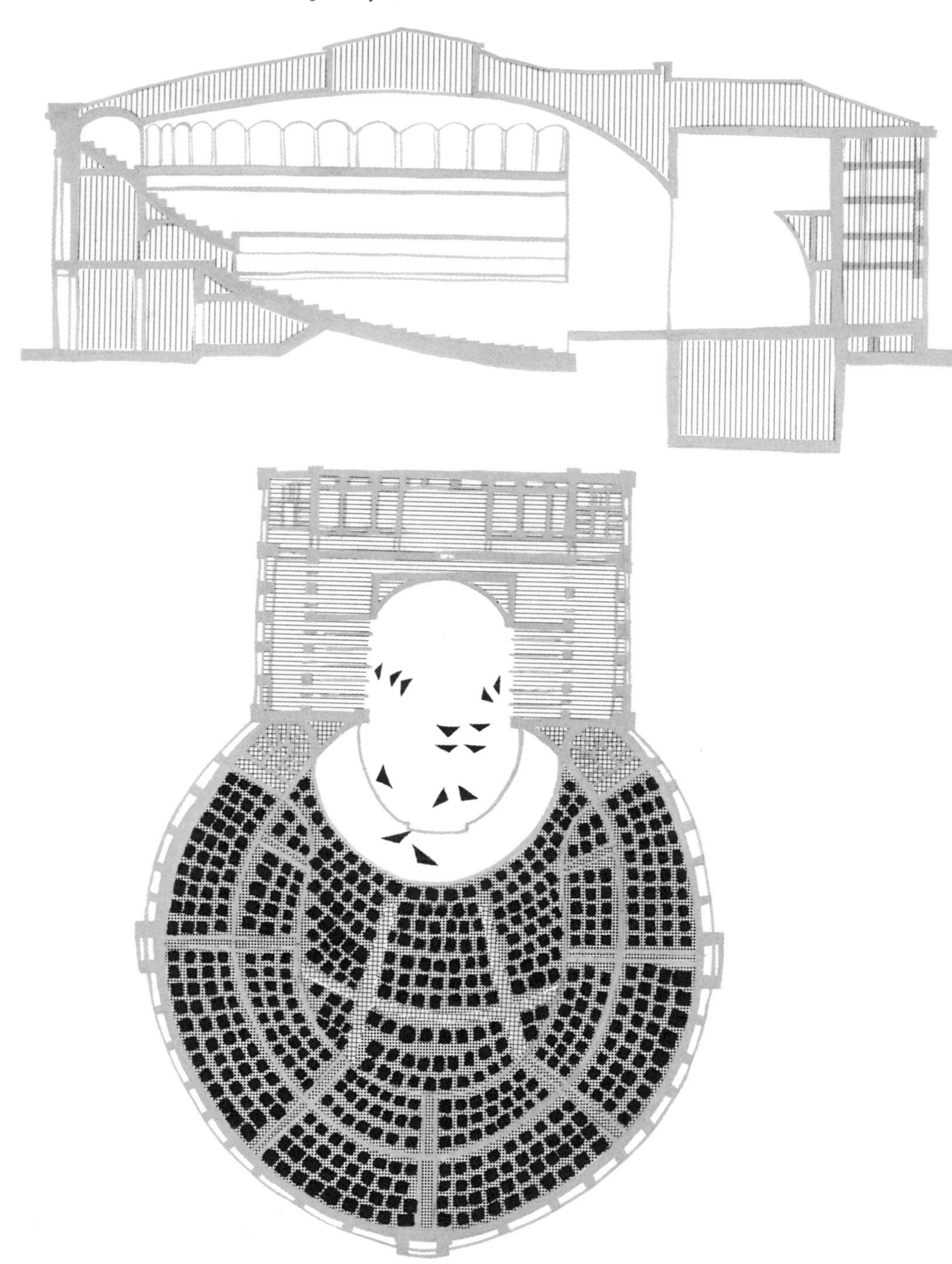

Figs. 18, 19. Davioud and Bourdais designed a refined seating plan with a "dish" shape that is still essential to sightline solutions for today's fan-shaped auditorium.

Gas to Electricity

The introduction of electricity during the nineteenth century was the first major technological innovation in the theatre since the Renaissance. First used in 1882 in London and Paris theatres, electric light was not only more controllable than the old gas lighting, but added a new palette of colors for designers. Colored light was used in borders and footlights, as well as in front-of-house spotlights, and it introduced a new kind of painted scenery to the stage.

The new electric light also affected the auditorium. General illumination in the auditorium with candlelit chandeliers and with gas mantles had been a necessity since, psychologically, hearing and intelligibility are improved when an actor's facial expressions and small gestures are clearly visible. As a consequence, theatre auditoriums had never been completely darkened during performances, and the contrast between the lighting onstage and in the auditorium had never been great. With the advent of brighter, controllable electric lighting, Wagner and Strindberg were soon to encourage darkening the auditorium in order to enhance the image on the stage.

This also had its effects on scene design. Electric light gave the three-dimensional box sets a truer appearance of reality, and settings became more and more literal. Designers added realistic ceilings and other literal details, which naturally required additional operational space and storage space backstage, as well as larger crews and stronger stage machinery to handle the bulkier, weightier scenery. So engineering ingenuity again came to the fore, leading to electrically movable platforms or wagons, elevators, and turntables.

Furthermore, realistic details affected the shape of the auditorium also. Since realistic ceilings on box sets were out of sight for people seated high up in the balconies, top balcony seats became obviously less desirable. A new direction in modifying the shape of the auditorium was sparked. So that the entire audience could appreciate all the new realism of the setting, theatre builders attempted to accommodate the top balcony seats on the orchestra level and in the first balcony, thereby enlarging those areas.

Nineteenth-Century American Theatres

In America, however, where the emphasis was on an expanding frontier, theatre design lagged behind Europe. Theatregoing increased, however. With the Industrial Revolution, more people were making more money. Enterprising merchants built "opera houses" in the new, fast-growing cities, whether or not music and drama were either available or popular, and by the mid-nineteenth century every medium-sized American town had at least one theatre structure, usually known locally as "the Opera House."

The design of these houses was loosely based on early nineteenth-century European theatres, before elaborate mechanization was introduced. American publishers even put out copybooks showing how to design "a simplified European opera house." And a few Italian and French decorators were brought over to make several theatres more "European" in appearance, if not in functional fact.

Unlike Europe, there were few local companies and no municipality- or government-subsidized companies. American companies were commercially self-sustaining. Depending on the size of the city, visiting Italian opera companies, touring circuses, or European Shakespeare troupes would be booked for limited runs. It became a prosperous activity, paying handsome profits to shrewd investors. The few resident symphony orchestras and grand opera companies were constantly subsidized by private donations.

With the exception of such established repertory companies, both producing management and theatre ownership were in the hands of entrepreneurs with a strictly business interest in theatres. They built their own theatres, provided their own production capital (sometimes paying enormous salaries for star attractions), and often made fortunes for themselves. Regrettably, almost none of these profits was reinvested in the theatre buildings themselves. Owners had minimal requirements when commissioning new theatres: "Get in as many seats as possible and let's not waste too much space on the stage or lobby or anything else." Few improvements were ever made to existing theatres—backstage or auditorium.

Nineteenth- and early twentieth-century American theatres, as

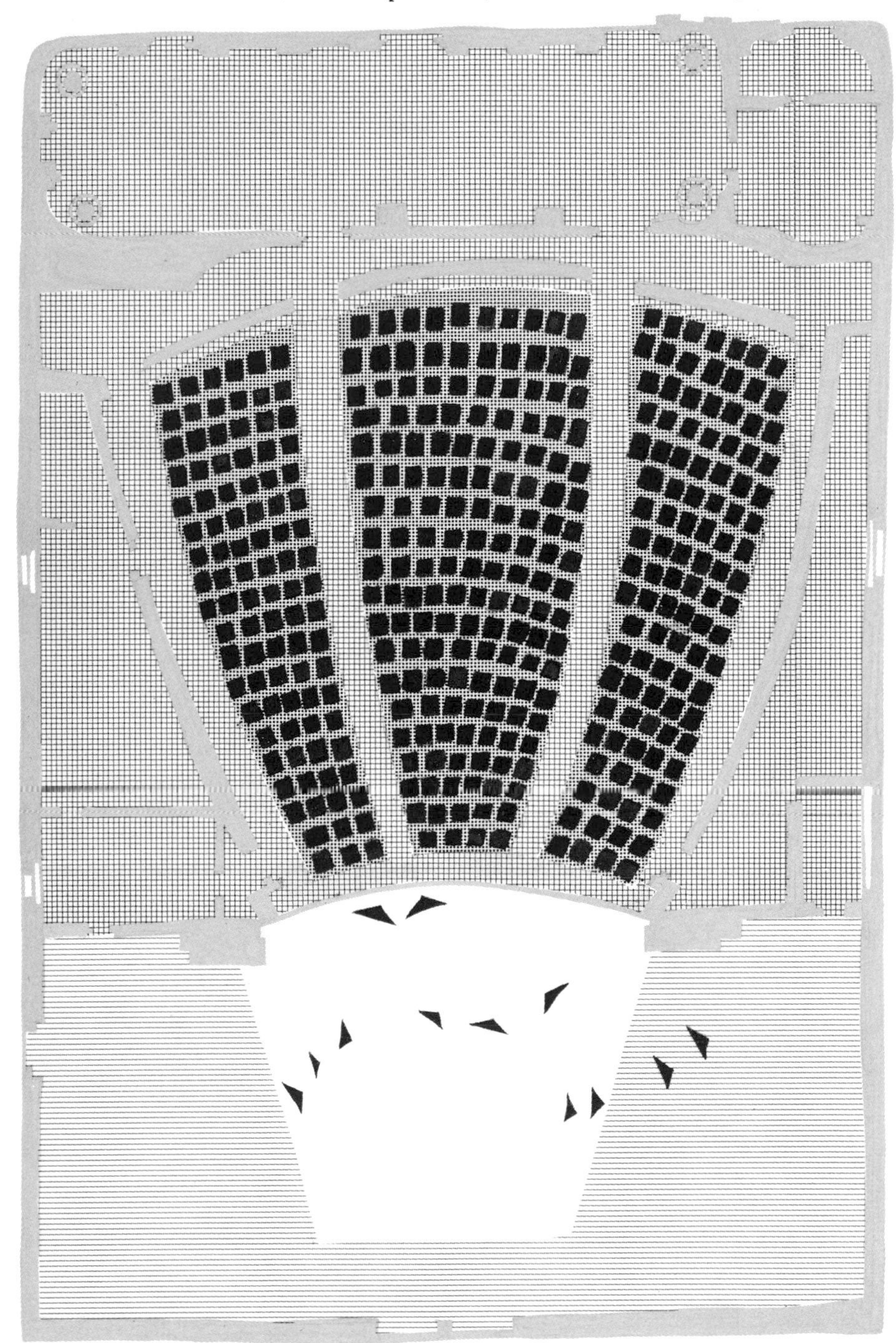

Fig. 20. Nineteenth-century American theatres, often called Opera Houses, were loosely based on earlier ninteenth-century European theatres.

a consequence, were not architectural gems. Local builders had little experience with theatre architecture and none at all with the technical needs of the theatres. Architects had little experience in theatre designing and small guidance from knowledgeable actor-managers in translating European culture for American economic and cultural needs. The sole exception was Chicago's Louis Sullivan, who with Dankmar Adler, designed in 1886 the elaborately mechanized Chicago Auditorium.

Most buildings were poor excuses for theatres, and so they remained until well after the beginning of the twentieth century. Even the larger, more successful companies—such as the Metropolitan Opera of New York—were far from enjoying the facilities of contemporary European opera houses. Inadequate space backstage added enormously to the heavy financial losses of opera repertory companies. It was to be more than eighty years after the building of its first home, in 1882, before the venerable Metropolitan Opera Company would have technically up-to-date stage machinery and adequate stage space.

Early in the century, one of the most significant influences on all the arts was the Freudian concept of the unconscious. Exploration of man's psychological inner world profoundly affected the fine arts movements—from Expressionism and Surrealism to Abstract Expressionism.

When dramatists began to explore the subconscious, they found the conventions of naturalistic writing and scenic realism too rigid. They rejected the constraining format of scenes and acts, moved toward multiple scene, flow-of-consciousness writing. Finding long pauses for slow scene-changing hampering, they made new demands on the stage technicians for immediate changes.

Directors and stage designers, at the same time, explored new mechanical and visual means to make these scene changes. New ideas—from Appia and Craig in the theatre, Picasso and Braque in painting, the Bauhaus and Le Corbusier in architecture—influenced stage-set design. Technicians used new backstage aids to complement the dramatists' unlimited scenic sequences.

The answer was multiple scene changes in full view of the audience; these liberated the theatre from rigid, three-act formats with long intermissions for scene changes. Better technical facilities were developed to carry out these onstage set changes.

Symbolic and suggestive scenery was revived, and imaginative lighting techniques were developed to express the drama visually. Projected light images were the most imaginative and fluid device. In Europe, theatres were already well supplied with all necessary equipment to develop stagecraft—turntables, elevators, stage wagons, ample backstage storage space, and available technicians. It was in these subsidized European repertory operations that the new stagecraft blossomed without inhibition. In essence, it was a return to the ancient techniques of changing scenery on a curtainless open stage; it was also the root of a revival to come.

IV

Multiple Choice in the Twentieth Century

The twentieth century brought an entirely new attitude toward shaping our theatres. Whereas in the past, a consistent, developing production technique gave rise to a single, if gradually developing theatre shape for each period, in the last sixty years several theatre shapes have been available for our use. Due partly, no doubt, to nineteenth-century historicism and scholarship, a revival of earlier stage forms sprang up to accompany the mainstream tradition of the Proscenium Stage. There began to be a multiple choice of theatre shapes for plays in the twentieth century—a situation that was unknown in previous times. This movement clearly underscored the tremendous activity in theatre arts—the thinking and lack of it—being done by all people involved.

Proscenium Theatres

From the turn of the twentieth century to the present day, the Proscenium theatre—a direct-line survival of the horseshoe opera house that originated in the Renaissance—has continued as the most generally accepted and widely built theatre shape in this country. By definition, a Proscenium theatre is a shape in which the audience faces the performing area on one side only and sees the performing area through an architectural opening that often has an elaborated architectural frame—although that is not an essential element. The performing area is not always limited by that opening; it can project out a nominal distance into the auditorium in the form of what is called a forestage or apron. In essence, this is not an intimate theatre shape, since the audience and the actors are each in separate, but connected, interior rooms.

At the turn of the century, many American Proscenium theatres were outmoded and run down, despite the fact that the theatre itself was prosperous. Unlike European theatres of the time, in the United States experiments were hampered by the lack of space, prohibitive labor costs, and the overriding profit motive of the commercial American theatre. Very few of these theatres were built with adequate machinery—stage elevators or turntables. Tenants were expected to bring everything with them, including turntables and all lighting equipment. Consequently, early twentieth-century producing groups dedicated to the new stagecraft and contemporary American playwrights found their theatres woefully inadequate in shape and meager in equipment.

The absentee landlord's profits were not put back into the buildings or into new equipment, particularly stage lighting equipment. Actually, landlords were not absent physically. What was missing was any real love of the arts of the theatre; instead

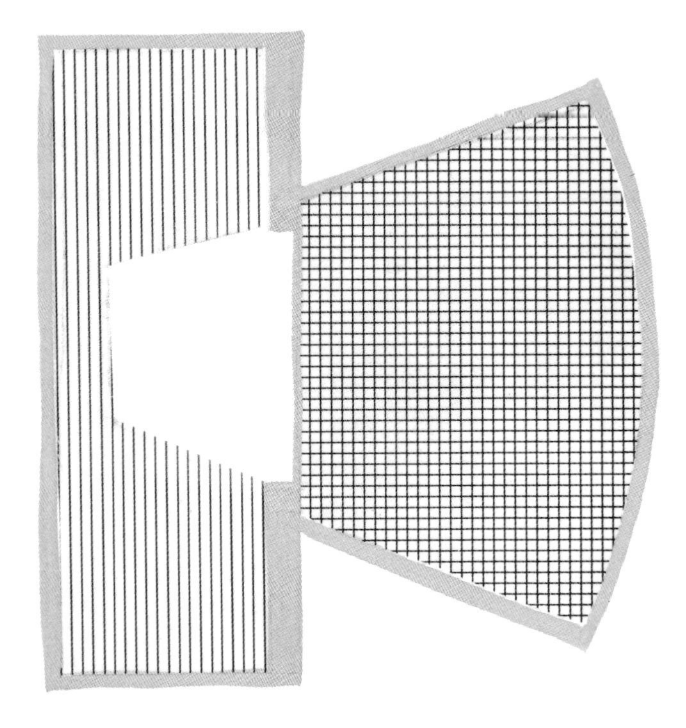

Fig. 21. The Proscenium shape.

Fig. 22. The typical early-twentieth-century American theatre had meagre and often inadequate stage and supporting facilities.

they substituted a love of profits. If they were away from their theatres for any length of time, their general managers were on hand to keep a watchful eye on financial operations.

One New York City landlord-builder ordered a theatre constructed with as little space as possible for the stage, the lobby, and between-legroom rows. In one instance the box office was omitted entirely. In spite of the owner's concern over his new theatre's capacity to operate on a profitable level, the absence of any professional theatre people on the owner's or the architect's staff was responsible for the amazing omission. Only in a last-minute inspection by the owner did this situation reveal itself, and a hastily designed and very cramped box office was quickly put in.

One theatre builder in Philadelphia forgot to include dressing rooms and later had them constructed in a separate building across an alley, back of the theatre. This little convenience meant that the artist, to get from his dressing room to the stage, had to go down to the basement, literally duck under sewage and steam pipes and then go up into the other building. All this showed little understanding for the art of the theatre—and no respect for its artists.

Because of this general situation, it was the producer, not the theatre owner, who was forced to keep up with the times and pay for proper facilities and equipment to install portable dressing rooms backstage. I note these almost unbelievable instances not in the spirit of gossip, but to stress the need for the constant presence of a professional theatre expert—not on the outskirts of a projected theatre design, but in a position of responsibility.

However, some producer-managers who were clients for their own theatre buildings had a real love of theatre itself, and an understanding of the latest European stagecraft developments. Among them were the Frohmans, David Belasco, and Florenz Ziegfeld; the latter retained architect-scene designer Joseph Urban to design his own theatre. Winthrop Ames, a wealthy amateur of the arts, and a thoroughly professional producer, put up the Century Theatre on New York's Central Park West. This 2,000-seat theatre was notably ahead of its time, but was soon demolished because no contemporary repertory company could fill it.

If the absentee theatre owners had been more knowing, if they had even more materialistic imagination, they would have made the kind of improvement that Billy Rose later made to his Ziegfeld Theatre (since demolished). There he equipped the backstage as well as the auditorium with the latest, most efficient lighting equipment and lighting control systems. Even if motivated solely by financial self-interest, this produced lucrative rentals from his tenants, and also provided presentational potential for the users.

Because the picture frame theatres were badly designed and therefore nearly unusable, they have recently been much downgraded. They were not bad simply because they were old or because they had Proscenium forms, but because of their initial poor design. What most of us have forgotten is that the Proscenium Stage has been for centuries and will remain one of our most useful theatre shapes.

A Revival of Ancient Shapes

As early as 1914, a group at Teachers College in New York used the simplest bleachers and seats on four sides of a medium-

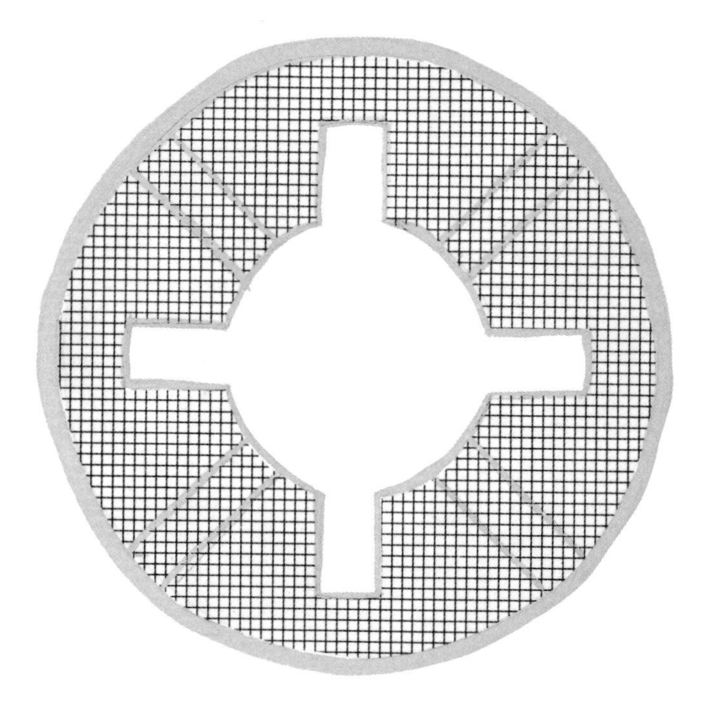

Fig. 23. The Arena shape.

sized room to create an Arena Stage. An ancient theatre shape, the Arena Stage was used in the great coliseums and arenas of Greece and Rome—but never specifically for drama. This new usage was the beginning of a revival.

The Arena is a theatre-in-the-round. The stage is surrounded on all sides by the audience. This arrangement puts the greatest number of the audience in intimate proximity with the performer. Both the audience and actor are in the same room. Others were gradually won to this cost-saving stage form which automatically minimizes the expensive, elaborate scenery usually associated with the Proscenium tradition.

The period following World War I was exciting both in Europe and America. Inspired by a fresh approach to writing and the new European expressionistic stage designers and producers—Adolphe Appia in Switzerland, Max Reinhardt and Leopold Jessner in Germany—our best young playwrights, Eugene O'Neill, Elmer Rice, and John Howard Lawson helped launch and stimulate a new attitude toward stagecraft in the United States.

Expressionistic scene development in Germany and Russia was also reflected in America. Lee Simonson, Norman Bel Geddes, and Robert Edmond Jones produced designs of dramatic imagination for scenery and stage. However, since they were not in the mainstream of commercial thinking, few of these new stages were actually built.

Conventional Broadway was not the only vital place; community and college playhouses sprang up all over the country. But the time and cost of producing scenery led directors to bypass that traditional problem and to investigate other techniques of stagecraft.

Early in this century, the ancient Open-Thrust Stage, which had been used before the development of the Proscenium theatre, was revived by several directors and producers. High costs of Proscenium productions, which required elaborate and sometimes complicated scenery as well as high operating costs, led to this revival. Coupled with this was a desire to bring greater intimacy to the theatre again.

The Open-Thrust Stage had experienced an earlier revival in Europe. Davioud and Bourdais' unexecuted 1875 opera house design proposed a stage of extreme thrust, extending fifty feet into the auditorium with seating on three sides. And in the

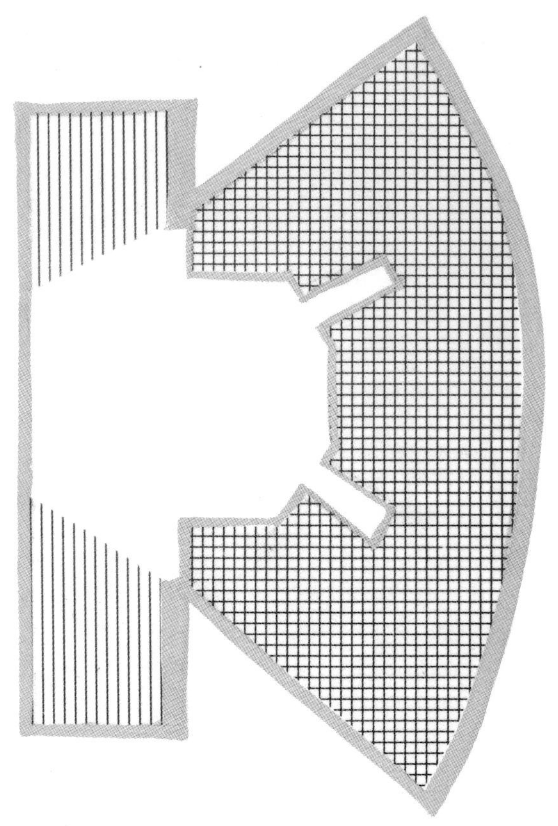

Fig. 24. The Open-Thrust shape.

twenties, the Parisian actor-director Jacques Copeau conceived a truly open theatre chamber of intimate proportions in his Theatre Vieux Colombier. His Open Stage had multiple levels, a number of entrances and exits, and a flexible architectural set, which was permanent and therefore cost-cutting. Neither of these European theatre designs directly influenced American stage designs, however, until the educational theatre did so much to spur the revival of the Open-Thrust Stage.

American educators felt that the proper method of teaching Shakespeare was to permit students to act and to observe performances of his plays on the type of stage for which they were written. Educators often attempted makeshift Open-Thrust Stages in whatever theatres were available to them. Scenery of the Proscenium tradition was virtually eliminated in Open-Thrust stagecraft. And ultimately permanent Open-Thrust Stage theatres were constructed by the producers of Shakespeare festivals for such re-

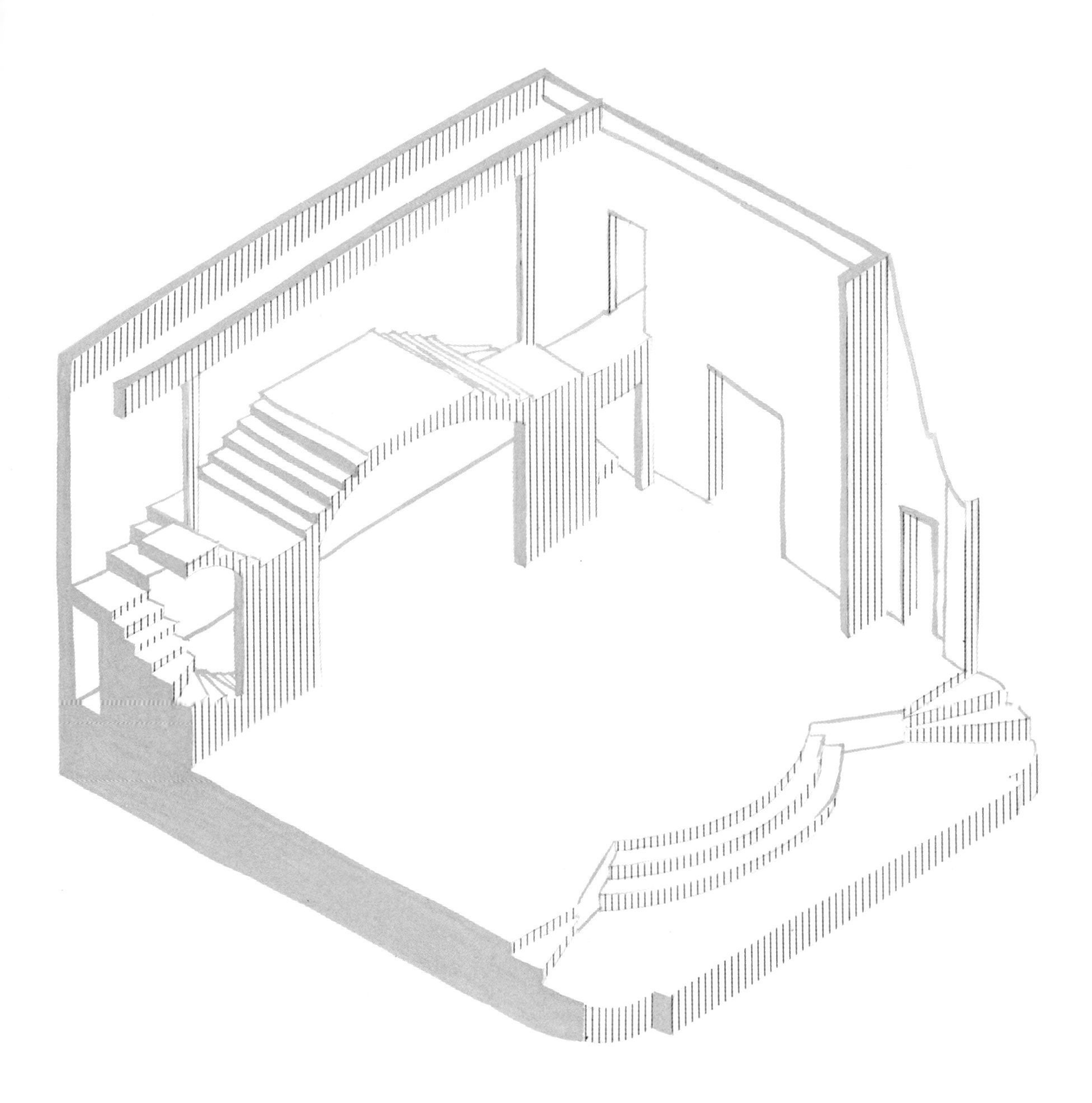

Fig. 25. The Open Stage of Jacques Copeau's Vieux Colombier, Paris, had multiple levels and a flexible, but permanent, architectural set.

gional and community groups as those at San Diego, California; Portland, Oregon; and later the Folger Shakespeare Library in Washington, D.C.

A Thrust Stage must not be confused with extended forestages in Proscenium theatres, which utilize techniques of acting, direction, and designing that do not differ from standard Proscenium stagecraft. A true Thrust Stage is a platform extending into an open auditorium in which the audience truly surrounds the stage on three sides. There may be exits in the back of the stage, as well as under the audience through vomitory tunnels. A Thrust Stage is an area deep and wide enough on which to play a full scene. When an apron or forestage is only an adjunct to a Proscenium Stage, it should not be considered a Thrust Stage.

Thus, by the end of the twenties, theatre professionals had a choice of not only the traditional Proscenium Stage, but also the revived Open-Thrust and the Arena Stage forms.

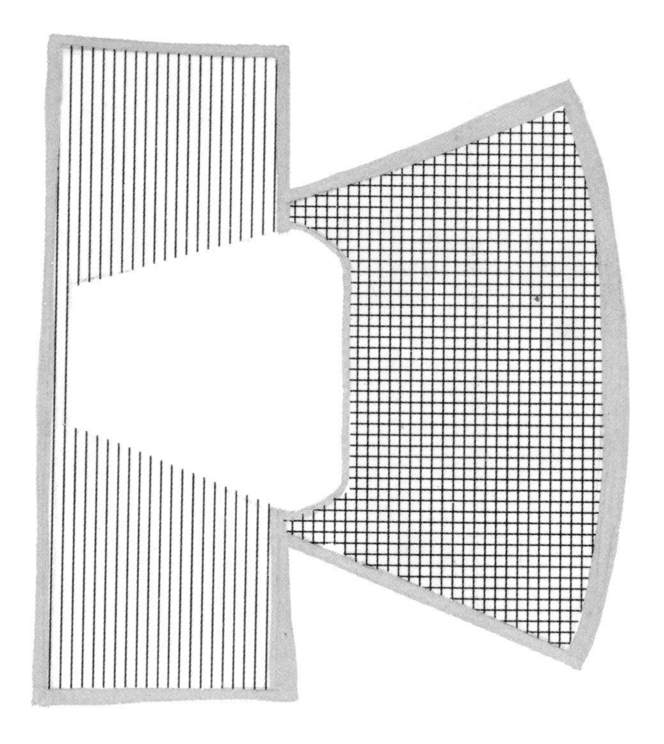

Fig. 26. The Apron shape.

Hiatus in Theatre Building

The Depression of 1929 brought a virtual end to theatre building in the United States until the end of World War II. No commercial theatres were built in major American cities between 1929 and 1950. The sole exception was Rockefeller Center's Center Theatre, built in 1936 and demolished in 1950. In the thirties, only a few colleges and universities had the funds to build modern theatres with stages designed for modern stagecraft and modern repertory requirements.

After World War II, America was ripe for a "cultural explosion." Mid-twentieth-century Americans were more affluent, better traveled, and more cultivated. There was a new boom in theatre construction, as we have described in Chapter I. The quarter-century hiatus in building, however, had left its mark. A whole generation of architects and designers had been passed by, and the new generation was unschooled in the development of stage design. This ignorance led to rampant confusion in theatre design.

Multiple Choice at Midcentury

When theatre building activity was resumed, the Proscenium was the only widely known theatre shape; therefore it continued to be popular. To make the Proscenium more effective for mid-twentieth-century use, new developments were introducd by architects and designers. Electrically operated flying scenery, electronic control systems like those that preset positions for stage elevators, and predetermined lighting plans made the designing of theatres as complicated as it made the physical operation simpler. More and more sophisticated attention to good sight lines and seating furthered the continuation of the Proscenium tradition.

Clients, on the other hand, sometimes continued a status-seeking reverence for seventeenth- and eighteenth-century European models that could not, in all ways, take advantage of these new techniques. A significant example of this reactionary view was the attitude of the Metropolitan Opera Board of Directors toward commissioning a new opera house in Lincoln Center. I am not criticizing the architects' designs or even their execution. The design was chosen with the conviction that the "Golden Horseshoe" of their old (1882) house was sacrosanct. A sentimental attachment to the past, as well as a lack of sympathy with contemporary design, may well have influenced the Board's decision. But I would suspect that the fear of alienating the small, but financially critical constituents was the dominant factor in their decision.

I am well aware that backstage the mechanical and electrical facilities of the new Metropolitan Opera House are up-to-date and undoubtedly do much to keep down the backbreaking operational overhead.

That they did not attempt to peer into the not-too-distant twenty-first century is understandable. The life-span of contemporary structures—particularly those associated with the performing arts, is shortening so quickly that new theatre shapes may serve satisfactorily for only a generation or two. But in deliberately choosing a multitiered eighteenth-century horseshoe seating plan, the directors were guilty of a graver error than just inflicting substandard sight lines. That error was the failure to recognize that our twentieth-century visual art forms are not just passing fads, but are deeply dyed in our daily lives, in our means of communication and our social behavior. It seems strange that the impresarios of an art form as abstract as music should allow themselves to close their eyes to even the most universally acceptable visual arts of our midcentury.

Today, only after careful consideration, proper planning and design will the Proscenium theatre regain its usefulness. A modern Proscenium theatre need not be rigid in its dimensions—either in width or height. Side panels adjacent to the Proscenium can have facilities for openings and side stages. Offstage rooms—right and left, up and down, traps and fly loft—all have to be provided. All these elements lend great flexibility to the Proscenium stage, but also make it more complex and more expensive to build. Basically, the Proscenium is one of the most flexible theatre shapes because any and all styles of production can be effectively realized. For the director, the problems of sight lines and other questions inherent in Proscenium productions are fluid. In stagecraft, particularly lighting and settings, everything from the most stylistic and simple designs to the most elaborate and imaginative

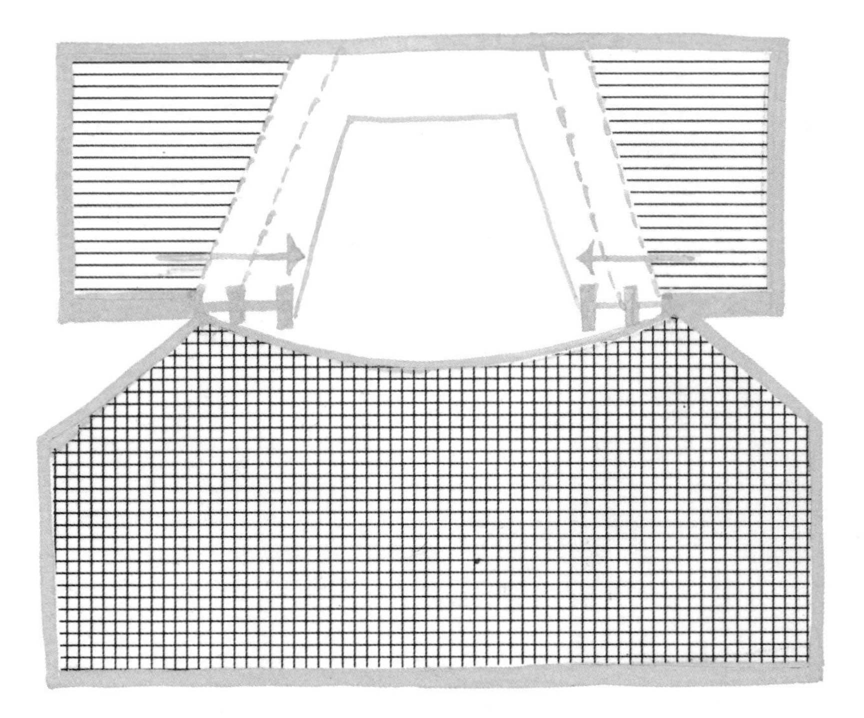

Fig. 27. In today's Proscenium theatre the width of the Proscenium opening can often be varied by adjustable panels.

settings can take full advantage of this shape. Even a play such as *Hair,* which was first performed on an Open Stage, was successfully produced on Broadway in a Proscenium theatre.

The limitation of this theatre shape is that it tends to be less intimate than either the Theatre-in-the-Round or the Open-Thrust Stage. Yet it also must be remembered that many playwrights want the kind of separation between actor and audience that the Proscenium shape gives. On the whole, if I were limited to a single stage form, I would choose a flexible Proscenium with an ample forestage.

During the 1950s, labor and material costs again led clients as well as producers and designers to seek new methods of stagecraft. So it was that Arena Stages or Theatres-in-the-Round gained wider acceptance as a suitable setting for spoken drama. They were less expensive to build and required virtually no conventional scenery. A strong influence during the theatre explosion,

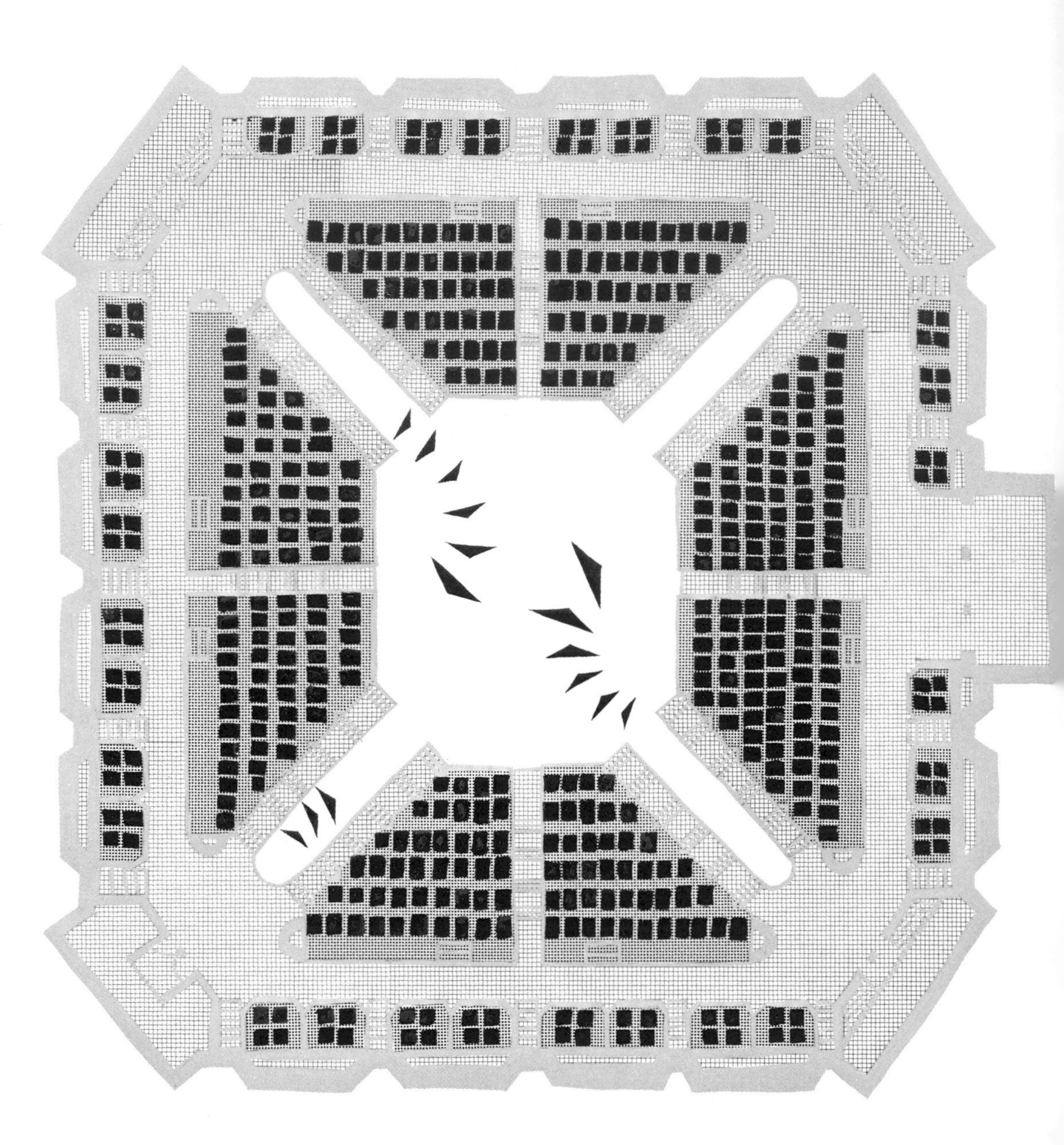

Fig. 28. The Arena Stage in Washington, D.C., designed by architect Harry Weese in 1961 is an exemplary modern Arena-shaped theatre.

the Arena Stage in Washington, D.C., clearly demonstrates how sophisticated Theatre-in-the-Round can be. Designed for Zelda Fichandler in 1961 by Chicago architects Harry Weese & Associates, it is a far cry from the frequently seen, makeshift Theatres-in-the-Round. Well planned and successful, it is actually a Theatre-in-the-Rectangle, but the principle of an audience surrounding the stage is identical. Here both the architect and the owner worked carefully to meet the needs of the company and to solve the technical problems and limitations of such a theatre shape.

One built-in limitation of Arena Stages is applicable to all stages surrounded, or partly surrounded, by the audience: the director must constantly change his axis to prevent one group of viewers from being presented with poorer images than other sections of the audience. Actors, as well as the director, must use entirely different attacks on performance and movement. Lighting is also more difficult in Arena staging because of the mandatory economy; however, when handled by an artist, this flexible medium can stress the nonillusionistic approach to a design.

In addition, the ability to vary settings is a limitation, both because architectural forms are impractical, and because elevations on the stage have to be limited in scale. In choosing a repertory for an Arena stage company, certain plays—such as the classical plays of Sophocles, Euripides, Shakespeare, Molière, and Sheridan—succeed while, on the other hand, some plays written for the Proscenium Stage must be omitted.

One of the primary advantages of an Arena theatre is intimacy. Even with 1,000 seats, the most distant member of the audience need not be much more than thirty-two feet from the nearest part of the stage. Although in more sophisticated Theatres-in-the-Round, it is possible to use traps and to fly elements overhead from a modified grid above the center of the stage, scenic investiture is ordinarily reduced to only the most expressive and economical forms of lighting and projection, costumes, props, and simple portable scenic elements that do not mask the actor from any part of the surrounding audience. On the whole, I think the advantages far outweigh the disadvantages of Arena theatres. The fact that presentation style stresses imagination and simplicity is surely a strong argument.

Throughout the fifties and sixties a major innovative force in theatre architecture has been Irish theatre director, Sir Tyrone

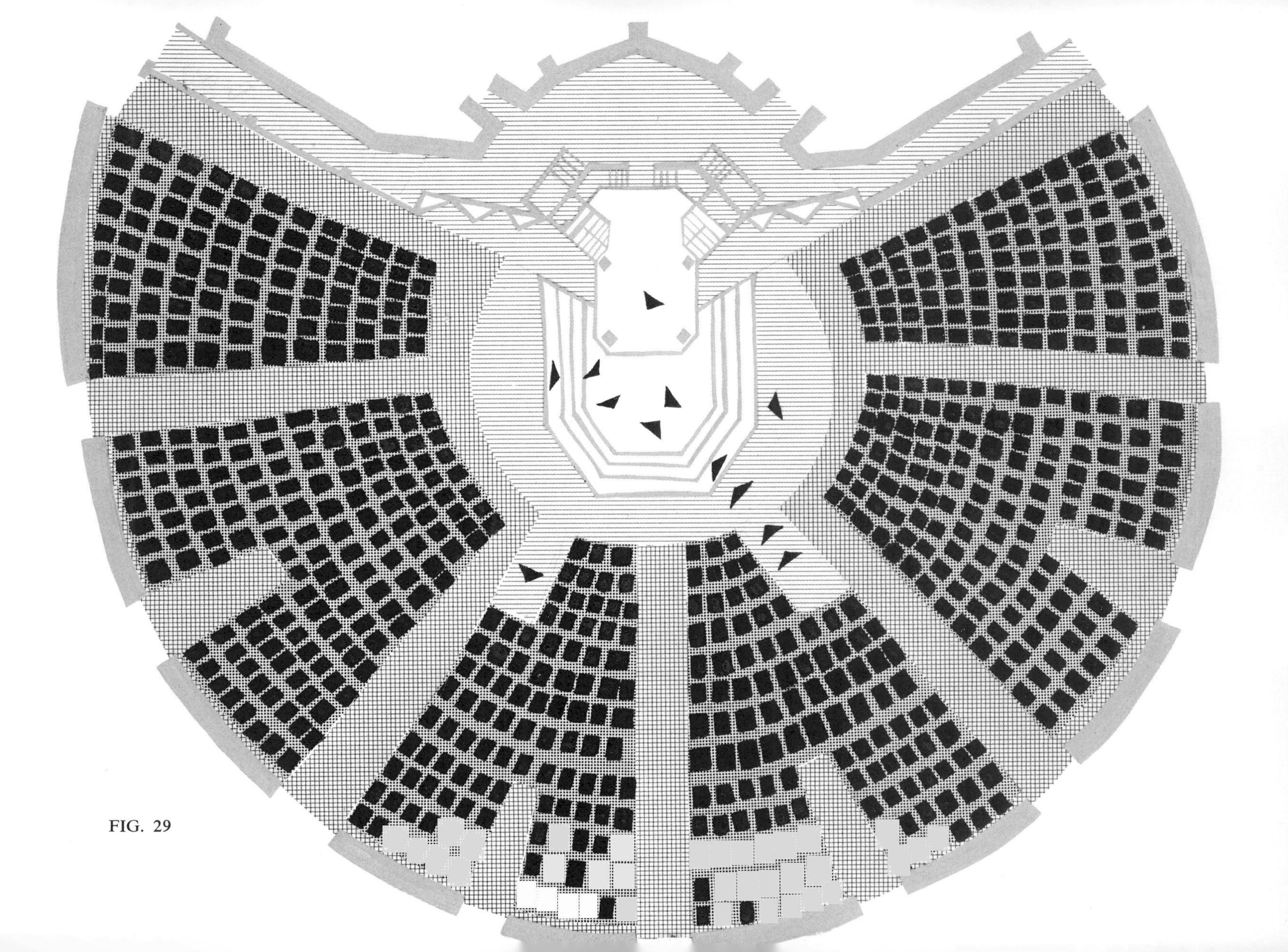

FIG. 29

Figs. 29, 30. The Stratford, Ontario, Shakespeare Festival Theatre has been an influential interpretation of the Open-Thrust Stage. It combines an Elizabethan Stage with a Greco-Roman audience seating plan.

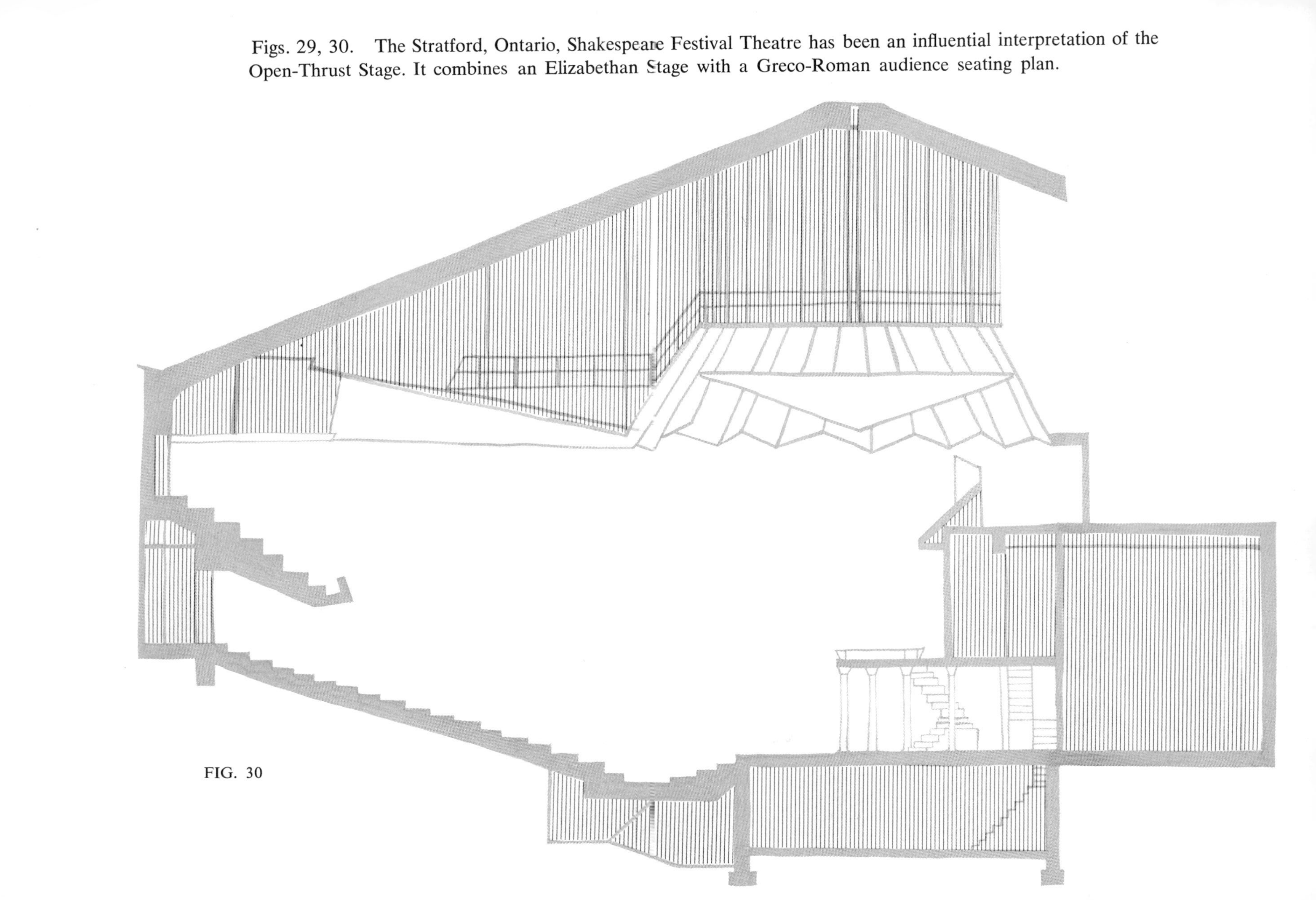

FIG. 30

Guthrie. In the fifties, after much acclaimed experimentation in England and Scotland, Guthrie was invited by the bright, ambitious young community leaders of Stratford, Ontario, to establish a theatre. Intended primarily for the classics, the theatre was first set up inside a tent, and later rebuilt under a permanent architectural structure.

Tyrone Guthrie's concept for Stratford, which was worked out with theatre designer Tanya Moisewitsch, was appropriately a classical one. The auditorium is based on a steeply banked, semicircular, Greco-Roman, three-sided seating arrangement; it surrounds an Open-Thrust Stage that has many basic elements of the Elizabethan stage. Besides entrances from the rear wall, Guthrie also used vomitories, which are entrances and exits to the stage from below the audience seating areas.

Little if any background scenery is used. Stress is on costumes, props, and lighting, which the director/designer team use in the most imaginative and simplest way to create scenic atmosphere. Light is used almost entirely as illumination, with very little sophistication in movement, color, or image projection. On the other hand, their sophisticated use of costumes and properties has been extremely important in creating a sense of mood and character. The impact of the theatre was international. It was intimate and vital, and extremely suitable for the classics.

A few years later, after the Ontario theatre had been built, Guthrie himself initiated, with Oliver Rea, a similar venture in Minneapolis, Minnesota. There, he planned with architect Ralph Rapson a variation on the Stratford, Ontario, theatre. Corrections were made, for example, in the sight lines at extreme left and right. He included facilities for hanging scenery behind the thrust. It is a token Proscenium behind the Thrust Stage. This combination of the two theatre forms was a major innovation. And thoughtful architects and designers throughout the country and abroad studied it with great interest.

An Open-Thrust Stage can be extremely simple, like Tyrone Guthrie's Stratford, Ontario, theatre. It can then be elaborated by planning an adaptable grid for lights, props, and scenic elements to be hung directly over the thrust. Yet all this fits into the basically simple staging that is germane to the shape.

The advantages of Thrust are clear and strong, but so are its disadvantages. Of the advantages, the greatest is perhaps the heightened sense of involvement gained by both the audience and the actor. Intimacy naturally is enhanced; the movement and pace of the play are swift; and the technique is fluid and cinematographic. The Open-Thrust Stage does, however, diminish the significance of the "illusionistic" style of stage design. (Depending on one's point of view, admittedly, this may be counted either as one of its advantages or as one of its limitations. For me, illusion is one of the lesser achievements of the contemporary theatre.) The Open Stage requires a totally different approach. The cast cannot be directed to act only toward the front, because the audience is on the sides as well. And, in a sense, they must act dimensionally within a scenic scheme, rather than in front of it. Costumes also become more important as do the few but choice properties with which the actors work. And finally, because background pictures are not being created, lighting must become a living element through which players move.

Generally, the Open-Thrust Stage is more flexible than the Arena. With the Open-Thrust Stage, the director does not have to worry so much about the actor's back being to the audience. But because the Open-Thrust is more complicated to design, it may turn out to be more expensive to build than the Arena or Proscenium theatre.

Perhaps the most outstanding disadvantage is that the more realistic a play is, the less effective it may be for the Open-Thrust Stage. Shakespearean plays and other earlier classics are easily adaptable since in their writing and production they were presented on Open Elizabethan Stages with a minimum of scenic effects. Much of nineteenth-century drama is considered ill-suited for the Open-Thrust Stage; but this also presents an opportunity for an imaginative director to approach these plays with a radically fresh style.

Of the multiple choices in theatre shapes at midcentury, then, three were prominent—Proscenium, Arena, and Open-Thrust; but more involved, complex choices of theatre shapes were yet to confuse the decision-making and design processes of architects and clients.

V

Multichoice in a Single Theatre

Besides the choice among three traditional, historical theatre shapes, which are available to theatre planners and designers today, a new combination of multiples has appeared. Now, we can attempt to have several, or all three of these stage forms in a single building—even in the same auditorium. This unique possibility has led to the extreme complication of present-day theatre design and to the utter confusion of present-day theatre designers.

The educator's desire to perform Shakespearean plays in the original setting has been extended to a desire also to perform eighteenth- and nineteenth-century plays in the theatres for which they were originally produced. Not content with an Open-Thrust Stage theatre for plays written for that basic shape, from the days of classical Greece to the Middle Ages, producers also want a Proscenium theatre, in which to present Renaissance and later plays. This desire has now spread from the educators to the producers of community and regional theatre as well.

Where sufficient funds are available, the building of two theatres—one Proscenium and one Open—splendidly accommodates this desire. (It must be remembered that in no age but our own were plays written expressly for Arena theatres.) However, sufficient funds do not always seem available for such a splendid solution. As a compromise, and it must immediately be recognized as that, architects, stage engineers, and designers have attempted to build, within a single theatre, Multiform Stages, which can be changed from one shape to another.

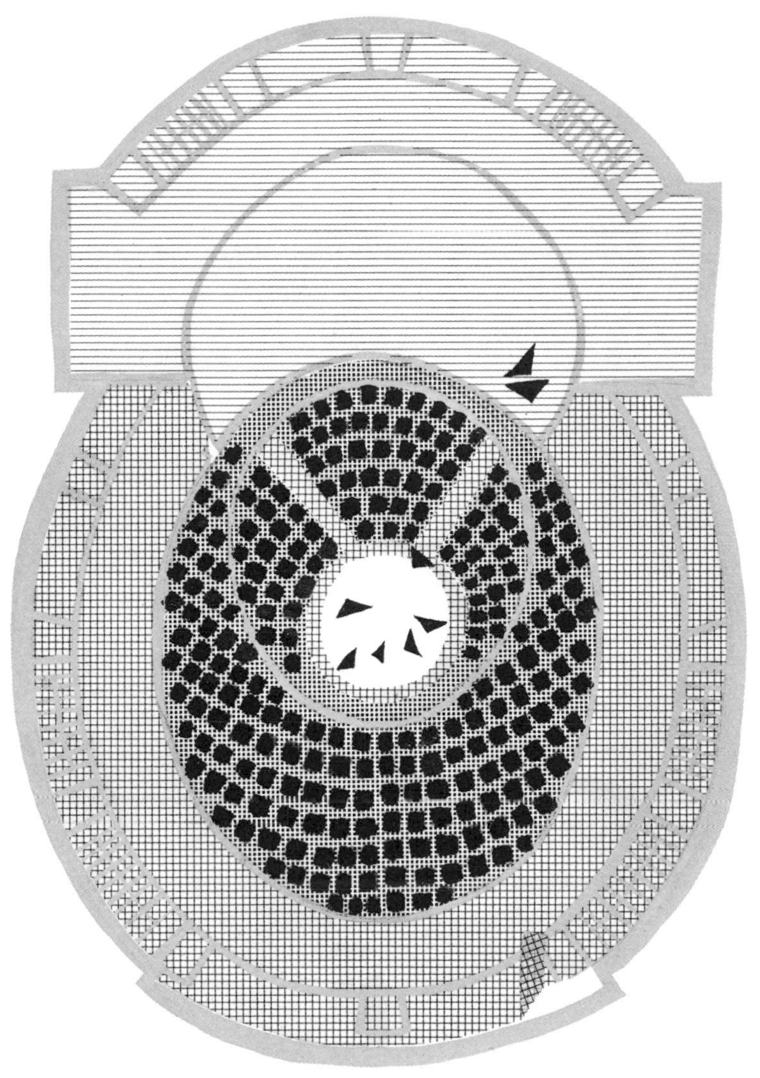

FIG. 31. GROPIUS THEATRE

The Multiform Stage

Inspired by the Total Theatre scheme of the late architect Walter Gropius, which was designed in 1929, but never executed, engineers have attempted tour-de-force theatres that could be altered from Proscenium Stage arrangements to Open-Thrust Stage arrangements—and even to the Arena shape. Engineering and mechanical ingenuity, coupled with accurate electric con-

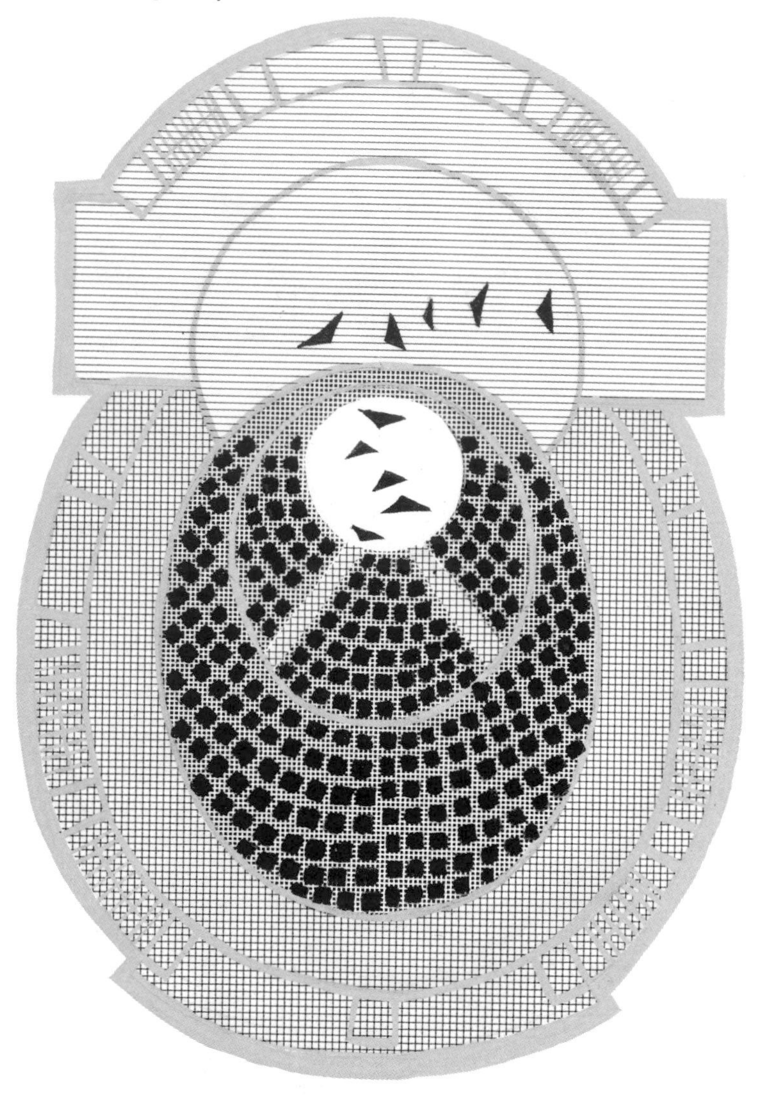

FIG. 32. GROPIUS THEATRE

trols, have made these chimeras appear attainable. It is my feeling, however, that this concept has never been successfully realized.

Multiform Stages were developed for clients who felt they could afford to build only one theatre, but were unable to commit themselves to a single stage form. The mechanical Multiform Stage was also intended to make flexible space operational for theatres of large size, and to save manpower and time in rearranging stage form and audience seating plans.

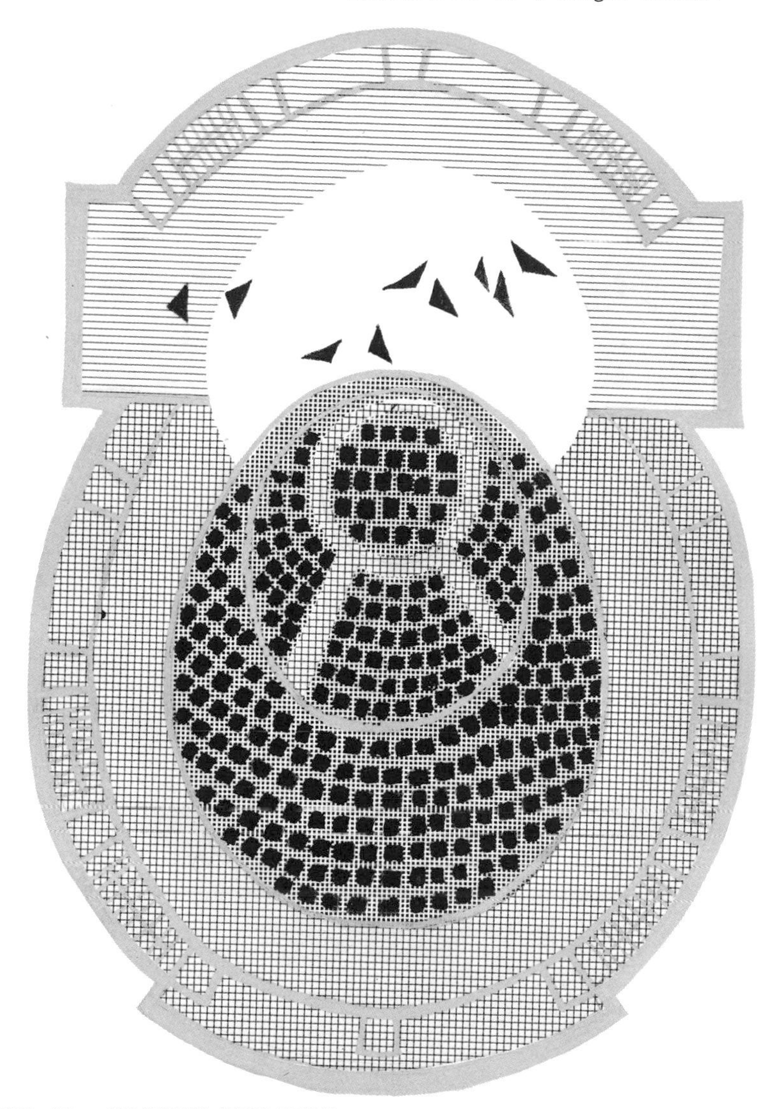

FIG. 33. GROPIUS THEATRE

Figs. 31, 32, 33. The Total Theatre Scheme, designed by Walter Gropius in 1929, is a chimera holding forth the illusive promise of a multiform stage. It could be changed from the Proscenium shape (Fig. 31) to the Open-Thrust shape (Fig. 32) and to the Arena shape (Fig. 33).

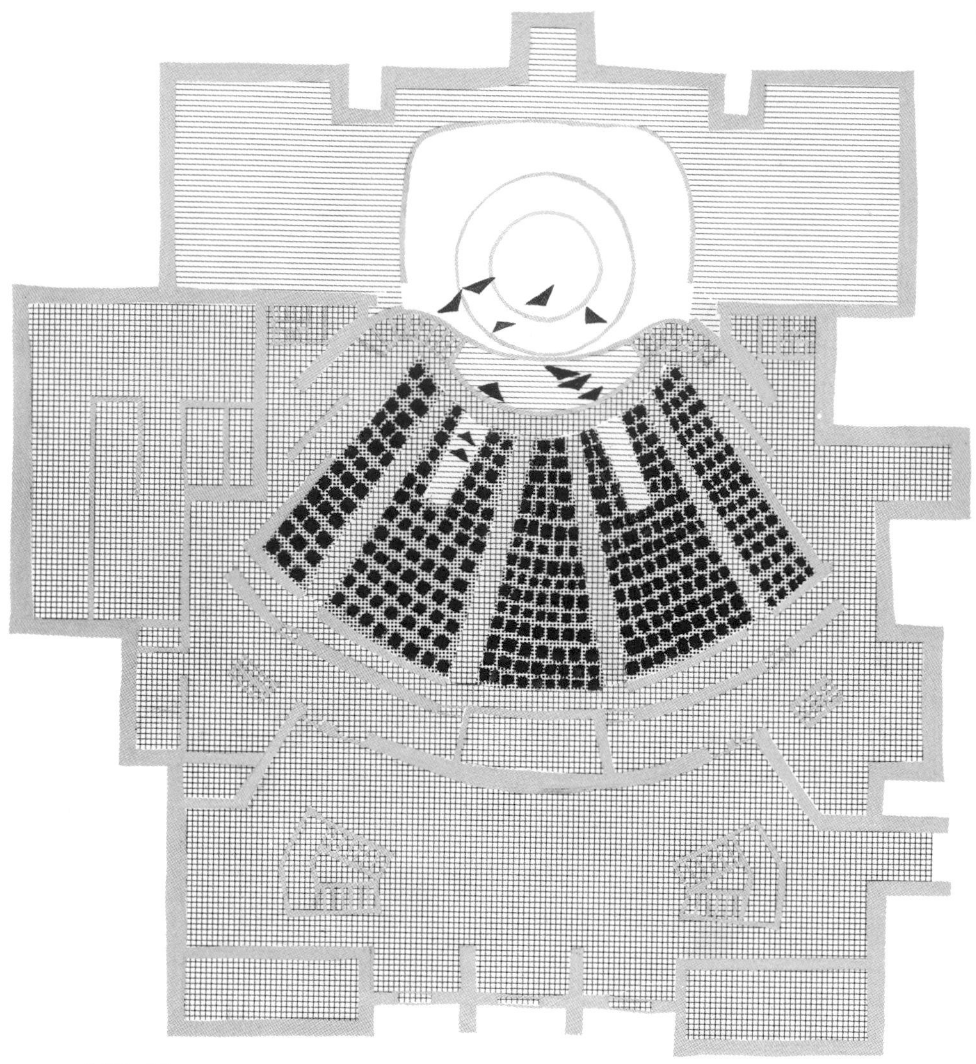

FIG. 34

In Figure 34 I have illustrated one theatre interior that can be used for two types of stage productions by rearranging some of the seating and changing the Proscenium proportions. The first is a true Proscenium technique. Then, by using an elevator to bring up a Thrust Stage and readjust the seating elements, this same theatre can be used for a second technique—the Open-Thrust Stage.

At the Loeb Drama Center at Harvard University, mechanical means have been provided to create three entirely different relations between acting area and audience seating. Designed by architect Hugh Stubbins and theatre engineer George Izenour, the Loeb Theatre interior itself does not essentially change—only the mobile units within its walls and under its ceilings. The avowed purpose of this highly selective and mechanical complex was to satisfy the needs of student directors, actors, and authors to create any and all stage shapes at will.

For all Multiform Stages, there is a price paid—not only in dollars, but also in sacrifice of function. No Multiform Stage can be either a perfect Thrust or a perfect Proscenium Stage. Yes, they work. But the additional expense, both in design and construction and ultimately in operational costs, is not worth the loss of unified purpose that characterizes a theatre with a single stage shape. Such experiments fail basically for the very reason that in none of their two or three or five alternate adjustments has one a feeling of a well-designed, simple, clean, direct, single-form theatre. In order to make a collective Multiform that works at all, each single arrangement must be a compromise.

It has been my experience that impressive and technically practical as some of the experiments may be, in none of their various chameleon-like changes are they as effective in either arrangements or elements as the stages designed for a specific purpose.

Even a theatre that can be changed to create only two of the basic stage shapes is a compromise. But such dual-form or "hybrid" theatres appeal to clients who desire some of the advantages of the Thrust Stage and, with a minimum of changeover, the use of the same auditorium as a Proscenium Stage. And it must be admitted that a stage that can be changed from Arena shape to Open-Thrust shape may not be so serious a compromise. The real difficulty is in designing a theatre that will accommodate both the axial vision demanded by the Proscenium Stage and the radial vision that is basic to the Open-Thrust Stage.

I have been involved (although after instinctive personal protest) in designing a number of dual-form theatres. An honest architect or designer must hold a Monday-morning quarterback session with himself, if not in public, upon the completion of an important job. I feel that a public session here will provide a valuable share of my experience.

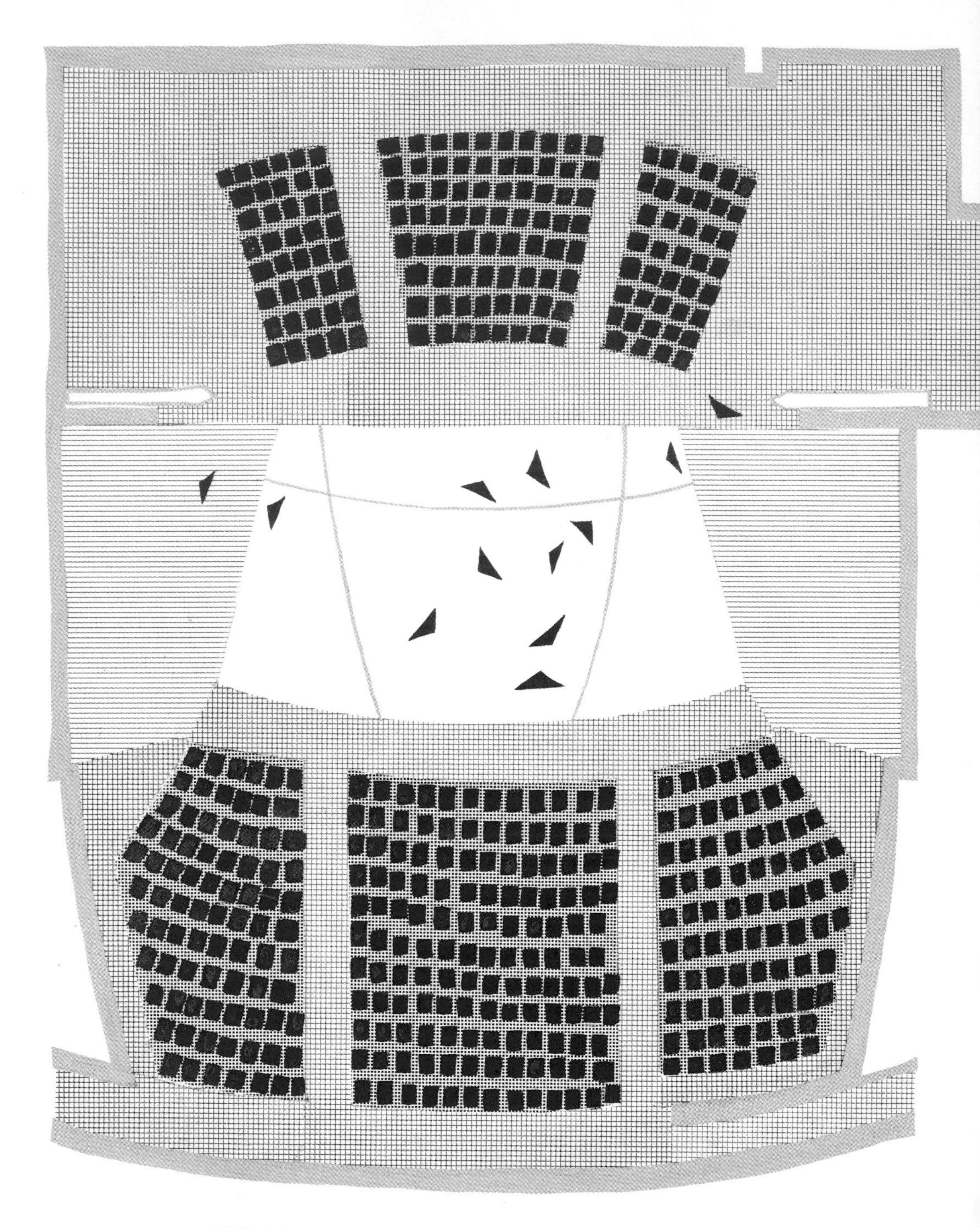

FIG. 35.

Figs. 35, 36, 37. The Loeb Drama Center at Harvard University, designed by architect Hugh Stubbins and theatre engineer George Izenour in 1960, is a small-scale realization of the multiform stage. Electrically

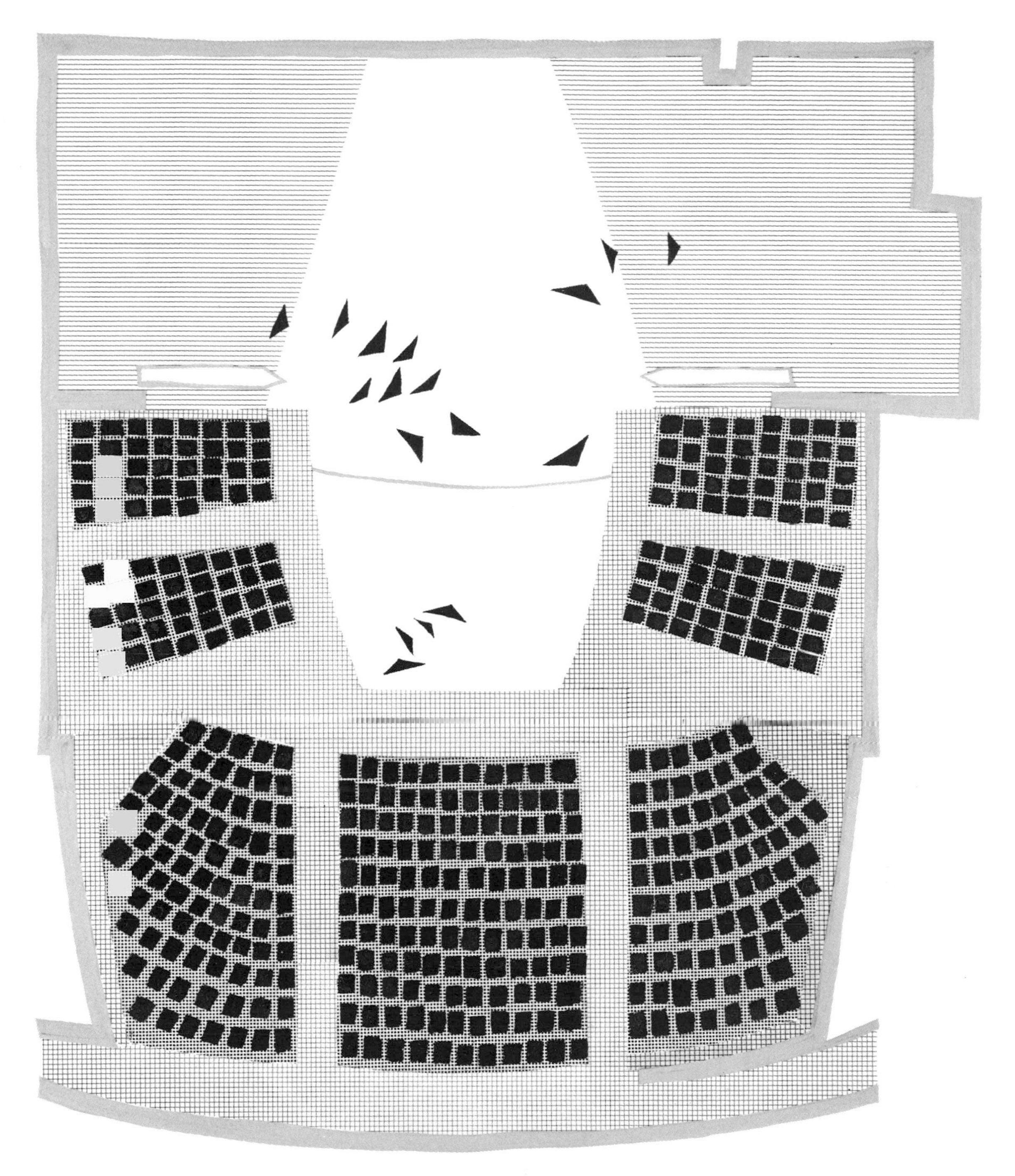

FIG. 36.

operated mobile seating units and stage sections can be rearranged to create a basic Proscenium shape (Fig. 35), a basic Open-Thrust shape (Fig. 36), and a modified Arena or Center Stage shape (Fig. 37).

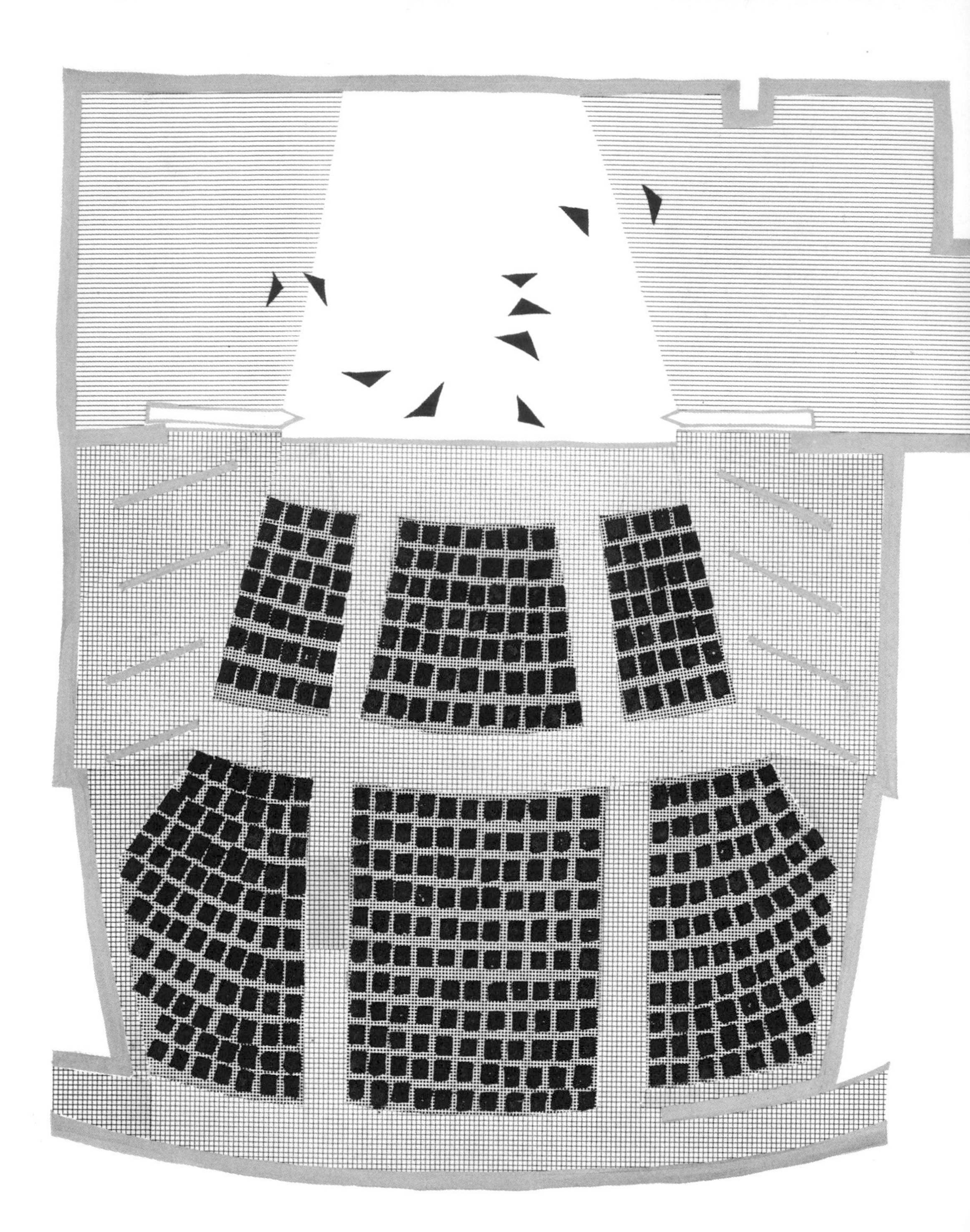

FIG. 37.

It was tragic that one of the great architects with a true and sensitive understanding of theatre, the late Eero Saarinen, should have lived to complete only the Beaumont Theater of Lincoln Center. It was a privilege to be codesigner with him on the stage and auditorium. When Eero and I were given the responsibility for designing the two theatres for the Lincoln Center Repertory Company, we met privately for long, honest studies. I found, to my pleasure, that our basic concepts were in agreement. First, neither of us believed in anything but single-form stages; we both were completely opposed to a Multiform Stage. If our original proposition had been accepted, we would have had the upstairs theatre slightly smaller and the downstairs theatre slightly larger. One of them would have been pure Thrust Stage and the other pure Proscenium. The question of which form would be which size would have been left to the building committee. That is, if the committee voted that the larger theatre should have a Proscenium Stage, we wanted that theatre to be a pure Proscenium theatre, in the best sense, and the other to be a pure Open-Thrust Stage—and vice versa.

We were overruled. In fact, some members of the committee even talked about a basic multi-use scheme for the Beaumont. We turned that down completely, but we realized that we would have to accept the compromise of a dual-form design. Our original proposition would have been the wiser decision, and ultimately far cheaper in both initial costs and in subsequent operating costs.

However, Lincoln Center gave us months of exploratory time and supported the costs of experimental designs and models which were shown to the building committee of the Repertory Company and to a group of theatre critics. A small, but very volatile minority of them supported the idea that the Open-Thrust Stage should be the dominant form. But at the end of the investigation, the consensus was that we should design the larger theatre so that it could be used as a Proscenium theatre and as an Open-Thrust Stage; and that we, as designers, should find some practical means of making the changeover relatively simple.

We pointed out that to meet the production schedule of a repertory company for a two-hour changeover between matinee and evening, it would be imperative to install expensive automatic mechanical equipment. For example, if a production using Open-Thrust was completed at five or five thirty and the evening

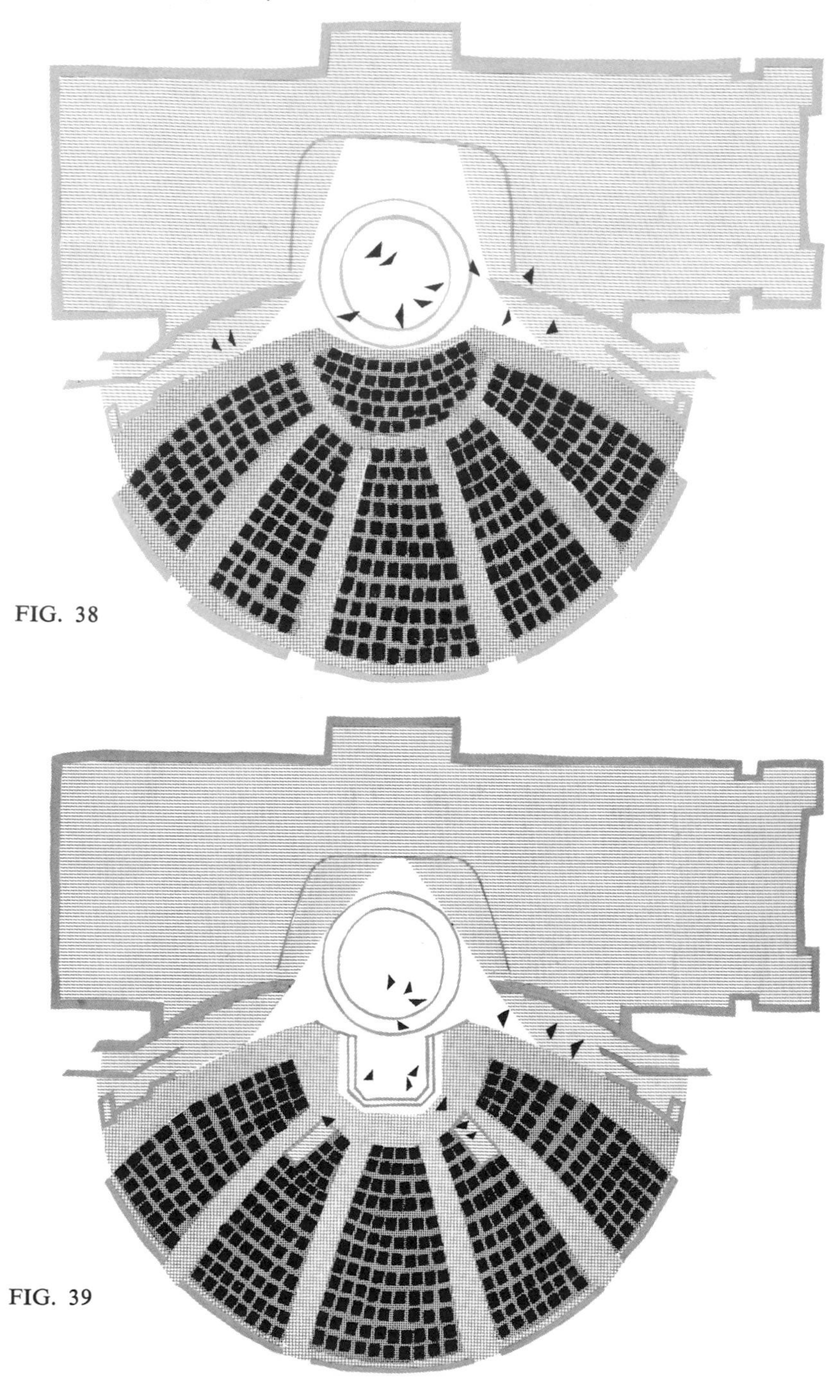

FIG. 38

FIG. 39

Figs. 38, 39, 40. The Beaumont Theatre at Lincoln Center, designed by Eero Saarinen and Jo Mielziner in 1960, can change its shape from an Open-Thrust Stage (Fig. 38) to a Proscenium Stage, with a modified apron (Fig. 39). The section (Fig. 40) shows a very deep stage planned schedule called for Proscenium staging, an enormous amount of work would be required not only in changing the scenery and lighting, but in changing the seating plan and the Open-Thrust Stage itself. What we designed at the Beaumont Theatre for this changeover can be effected in two hours.

It is achieved by locating the front group of seats on a large lift that descends to the subbasement where a turntable rotates them, substituting an Open-Thrust Stage, which is then raised into position. Proscenium panels at the Beaumont can be opened to make a maximum Proscenium opening that is fifty feet across. When the Thrust is in use, the panels are completely closed; then actors can enter from right and left downstage of the Proscenium panels and from two vomitory entrances under the front orchestra seats.

It must be stated categorically that Multiform Stages are designed for dramatic productions of plays only. In the case of the Beaumont, the acoustical characteristics are specifically for the spoken word. The theatre cannot be used successfully for opera or musical recitals.

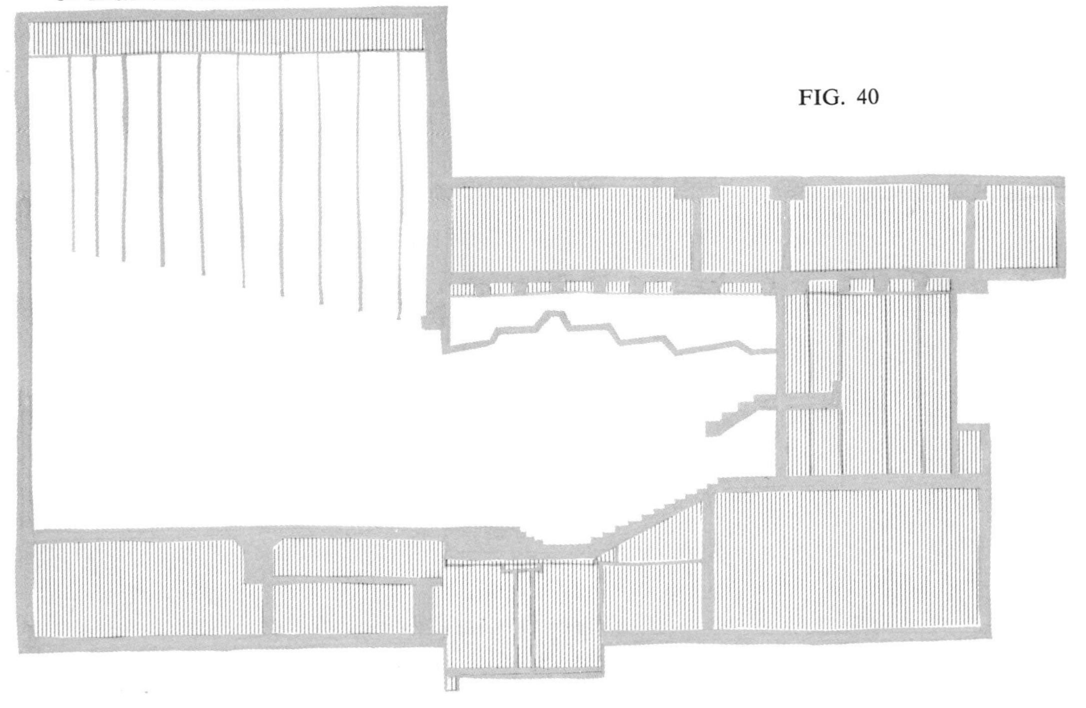

FIG. 40

for a repertory schedule. The deep stage, combined with large stage wagons, and a "saturation lighting" system as well as the multiform stage mechanism make it possible to change stage shapes and scenery from production to production in a matter of hours, with minimum labor.

Multi-Use Auditoriums

An approach to theatre shapes born of the mid-twentieth-century electronic era, and perhaps twentieth-century indecision is the Multi-Use Auditorium. It is an attempt to satisfy the client who wants an auditorium so adaptable in relationships that any and all the performing arts can be accommodated. Not only do performing groups want a theatre to house plays, but they also hope to use their new auditoriums for opera and musical productions, concerts, and recitals. But music reverberation time demands a greater spatial volume than that for the spoken word. What results is an attempt to build one hall that can be suited to both music and drama by altering the very volume of the auditorium. This implies large-scale physical changes being made to ceiling elements and even to the side walls of the auditorium. In some instances, an entire balcony can be shut off for the purpose of changing both acoustical characteristics and audience capacity.

Colleges and universities have led the race in building such facilities. High schools have built structures that attempt to accommodate the basketball court, as well as the performance of Ibsen and the choral society recital. Combinations such as the gymnatorium and the cafetorium have been tried as a means of saving space and construction funds. Such schemes appealed equally to builders, architects, and engineers, as well as clients. The Multi-Use theatre thus spread to fantastic degrees. And it has become a byword of confusion in the 1960s. Not only the idea, but the definition of the words, Multi-Use or Multipurpose, have become confused, even by theatre experts.

It is understandable that members of boards of trustees or college regents cried out for a single design to meet all the needs of all the performing arts. Even in affluent times, it is not easy for a large university or regional theatre group to raise enough money to build more than one good theatre. And there will inevitably be an avid army of architects, engineers, and acoustical specialists willing to take on that challenging desire of clients to accommodate all the performing arts in a single auditorium. Even when the architects or consultants are men of integrity and theatre experience, they may find difficulty in persuading building committees that however well an auditorium may suit the combined needs of the choral society and the music school opera, it cannot possibly be used for intimate drama as well.

This is when the dangerous plea is made to bring in the engineering magic that we see in so many regional and college theatres today, and in such community auditoriums as the Jesse Jones Hall in Houston.

During the 1960s, engineering firms devised astounding mechanical systems that changed the very shape of an auditorium, pitched the floor, tipping the ceiling and cutting off the balconies, pivoted the walls, and rolled banks of seating across the floor and stage. In too many of these cases, these electronic tails wagged the theatrical dogs.

Not all engineering developments were futile, however. Certainly in terms of stagecraft, electronic controls for rigging and lighting systems, which were often developed for such auditoriums, have been astonishing in their programs of complicated presentational problems, but these are mechanical contributions to the backstage area and are not to be confused with the mechanical manipulation of the architectural front-of-the-house arrangements.

It is certainly human on the part of an owner or manager to feel than a single auditorium with adjustable elements serves in place of what might otherwise be a complex of two or three separate theatres. But every medium in the dramatic and musical arts cries for a specific scale for the performing area and the audience. With the spoken word in drama, the sense of intimacy is essential both visually and aurally. Add music and singing from a musical comedy, and the scale of the auditorium can increase appreciably.

An auditorium that is good for the actor's voice is technically ineffectual for the singing voice and for musical instruments. The reverse is equally true. On an everyday level, we know that when we want to say something intimate to a friend, we do not shout it across a courtyard. We approach closely, eye to eye, and speak quietly in close contact, as in intimate drama. If we want to sing an aria to that same friend, we would back away or choose a room of sufficient size. The same principle holds in choosing a theatre shape.

Specifically, the distance between the last viewer and the performer can increase because when acting is augmented by broader techniques, the audience can be much farther away from the performer and still enjoy an acceptable contact. From operetta to grand opera, an even greater change in scale is acceptable. In fact, the patron who enjoys second-row-center seats at a drama would find grand opera completely unacceptable at this close range. To many followers of opera, of course, the aural appreciation is almost complete without the visual.

The scale that I have been referring to is not only the distance between the audience and the forestage, but also the width of the playing stage or Proscenium opening. As an example, a good width for a legitimate play is not much more than thirty-five feet; whereas opera stages will open sixty to eighty feet in width.

It is self-evident that the solution to housing all these art forms in one building must be a magic one, if technically successful. Furthermore, this technical magic must be a dominant part of the basic design. The Multi-Use Auditorium is one of the most serious mistakes in the history of theatre design. The notion that any single design can be used for all purposes is nonsense.

Uncommitted Theatre Spaces

Still another theatre design approach that developed during this period of "theatre explosion" is one for which there is no historical precedent in the tradition of our indoor theatres. It is based on the idea that neither of the basic elements that make up a theatre—audience or stage—should be predetermined so far as their location or configuration within the theatre are concerned.

In effect, this concept says that within the space provided by the architect, an undetermined stage area and seating area may be set at will in a wide variety of relationships, arrangements, and relocations. This final theatre concept goes one step further than the mechanized theatres. It rejects any and all means for creating a specific playing area or an audience area. Its proponents say, "Give me a cocoon that shuts out the outer world, and in it we will create our concepts without the aid of predetermined form." They feel that it frees future theatre users from any "set interior arrangement." They also proffer what they feel is the advantage of a simultaneous and multiple approach to dramatic problems. Theirs is the "Uncommitted Theatre Space."

Back in the 1890s, the great scenic artist Adolphe Appia said, "Let us abandon theatres to their dying past, and let us erect simple buildings instead, merely to cover the space where we work—no stage, no amphitheatre, only a bare and empty room." This bold pronunciamento, like many manifestos, bears some analysis. Any serious student of the theatre who admires Adolph Appia's magnificently conceived stage settings knows, however, that to achieve the subtlety of his mood lighting and the perfectly proportioned grandeur of his plastic forms, the most complex and technically sophisticated equipment must be available. Much of this equipment must be located not only backstage but in the auditorium itself and subtly related to the stage area. In other words, Appia's "bare empty room," once equipped to meet the high standards of his production concepts, would lose all semblance of nudity and emptiness and might become a well-conceived and carefully predetermined theatre.

The limitations of mechanized Multiform schemes are even greater in these uncommitted theatre spaces. On the economic side, the budget for such an indeterminate theatre must be greatly increased for purely mechanical equipment, if for no other. In order to justify the alleged freedom, a maximum amount of mechanical support must be available in every corner of the uncommitted area. Naturally egresses and exits, ventilating and heating equipment, supporting technical elements and power outlets for lighting must be predetermined and fixed. And the operating costs for moving this equipment are major restrictions on the alleged freedom.

Any rational study of the intricate problems relating to sight lines, acoustics, or lighting must also lead one to the conclusion that to keep these relationships in an undetermined plan can mean only that the ultimate quality of any single interior relationship is bound to be below par.

The only logical justification for this nonmechanical, multiform approach is for a university that offers a course in theatre architecture. As a really effective working laboratory for the study of acting, direction, and stage design, it is one to be researched and explored.

Uncommitted Spaces for Involvement?

Another current trend in stagecraft is the desire for even further involvement of the actor and audience. I refer to a greater psychological and physical contact between audience and actor, and to a greater use of sensory as well as visual involvement throughout the theatre. It has been suggested that the Uncommitted Theatre Space fosters this involvement.

Ever since the 1900s, nonobjective and totally abstract experiments in the arts have been expressed beyond the painter's and sculptor's studio. Changes in all communication arts—written and visual—have influenced dramatists in a revolutionary way. Poetry, prose, and journalism have all been affected by the tempo of the radio, recorded music, and their extension into cinematography and television. Poets have rejected rhyme, meter, and syntax. Prose writers have made equally insurrectionary demands on their medium. In the first fifty years of this century the theatre reflected very little of this movement. In recent years, avant-garde writers and directors have plunged into radical experiments in what they felt was a new theatre-oriented field that furthers audience involvement.

When I refer to total involvement, I do not mean what is currently referred to as a "Happening." The talk about Happenings is based on a valuable instinct—the genuine desire for greater contact, for greater participation of both audience and actor, but it is practiced and preached in an undisciplined and, I think, uncreative way. It is undisciplined because it makes a point of the fact that there is ostensibly no premeditated play, no rehearsal, no restrictive texts.

Although the charade, the conversation, the story, and the extemporaneous narrative have value, they are not basically theatre. Any theatre form—like all serious art forms—is born of deliberation, self-discipline, and creativity. To rely on improvisation, no matter how talented the actor, or how receptive the audience, is to misunderstand freedom.

Freedom in art is not license. The artist can be free only if he masters and accepts the limitation of his medium. I have always believed that authors and directors must be given the greatest freedom in staging. In the auditorium and on the stage, the greatest range of lighting, scenic equipment, and spatial freedom must be available. If a new play needs one hundred different visual indications of mood and background, it must be provided.

I have worked with directors and authors who desperately wanted to be free of any set format. But gradually, to have effects, lights, and scenic elements meet the needs of an actor at a precise moment, we started to reintroduce a theatrical limitation—dramatic form.

Similarly, we must accept and work with the physical limitations of our stages. If I have a stage that is only ten feet deep, and I want to give the impression of unlimited space, I accept that ten feet and do something with it. Suggestions and implications, whether they are visual, oral, or aural, are means of working with one's limitations. It might be the use of the magic of poetry or of music's abstract sounds. The power of the creative artist is infinite, but only when he masters the technique in which he creates. Yet all these production aids, these minute details, must be made practical and must be carefully timed and rehearsed. All the environmental background, born in excitement and high imagination, must be transposed into controlled and disciplined technique.

I feel I must state that I am not, on principle, anti-Happening. It must be said on behalf of Happenings that they do accentuate some of the better trends fostered by all contemporary dramatists and stage directors. They have one outstanding characteristic in common with other modern theatre movements—the desire to accentuate actor-spectator relationships.

The advocates of Happenings question the accepted concepts of actor-audience spatial relationships. Michael Kirby states in the *Tulane Drama Review* (Vol. 10, No. 2, p. 40, Winter, 1965):

> Performance and audience are both necessary to have theatre. But it might be thought that it is this very separation of spectator and work which is responsible for an "artificiality" of the form, and many Happenings and related pieces have attempted to "break down" the barrier between presentation and spectator and to make the passive viewer a more active participator. At any rate, works have recently been conceived which, since they are to be performed without an audience—a totally original and unprecedented development in the art—might be called "activities."

It would be pointless at this early stage of the avant-garde experiments in Happenings even to suggest what formalized theatre shape they might take, or if they will have any influence at all on theatre shapes. Their most vocal leaders seem to disagree about the best environment in which this new and exotic hybrid will flourish.

At this writing, this theatre of protest does find what seems to be adequate housing in a large variety of structures—both in and out of the theatre. So varied are they, that this particular form of dramatic expression does not easily fit into this discussion of theatre shapes. If and when it matures into a new art form, then it may develop a stage shape and auditorium especially designed for its own needs. I doubt that it will be a totally Uncommitted Theatre Space.

VI

The Program

Every theatre—educational, amateur, Broadway, subsidized or commercial, good or bad—has specific needs and a particular set of requirements. All these requirements, which ultimately will determine shape, must be carefully considered and set out in a program by the program committee. A written document that can be referred to like the Constitution, a program is normally executed in two phases: the first called "preprogramming" in which the preliminary planning is considered, and the second called "programming" during which the final and fixed requirements are delineated and written.

The preliminary program should be a statement in which the needs and aims of the theatre are clearly and definitely outlined, and approved by the owner-client. It need not be long or detailed, but it must state what the building should *not* be expected to accomplish, as well as what it will be designed to do. It should state a preference, not necessarily inflexible, for one of our contemporary theatre shapes. From this starting point, the program committee, the architect, and the overall theatre consultant then develop the final program.

The final program must be much more than a guideline. It gives definite instructions to create an atmosphere for the designers. It also must be specific in delineating the technical activity that will take place in this technical structure called a theatre. It must propose the minimum number of square feet for all primary and supporting theatre areas. It must state the function of each area and the priority of relative location.

The program must be written by the ultimate users of the theatre, or by the present users of an existing facility. Not to do so is to court failure for both the architect and the theatre. In the past, the programs that clients have submitted are often abysmally lacking in their delineation of the essential needs of the theatre. By contrast, an architect in a provincial city in Western Europe would be given hundreds of pages on the requirements of the potential users of the theatre.

Building programs that are hastily and not thoroughly thought out have sometimes forced costly changes to be made after preliminary drawings had been completed. A preliminary program turned, for example, into one-eighth-inch preliminary drawings can be taken by the architect to estimators who can arrive at realistic figures. If, at this point, the committee finds they are half a million or two million dollars over their budget, the preliminary sketches (rather than finished working drawings that would then be obsolete) can be restudied. Secondary elements can be amended, simplified, deleted, or omitted. A building committee that does not deal realistically and knowledgeably with theatre architecture and economics can allow enthusiasm to carry them far beyond their clients' ability to pay.

The basic decisions of a final program are the determination of audience seating capacity (first consideration); then the choice of stage and auditorium shape; next the size and number of specific supporting facilities that will be designed for stage, audience, and administrative staff; and finally, the equipment that will be included in each of these areas. The final program must take all these points into consideration.

Determining Audience Capacity

What do "large" and "small" mean in terms of audience capacity? Greek theatres often held ten thousand spectators. Medieval mystery and miracle plays were produced in the great cathedrals and in the marketplaces. The word "opera house" usually suggests a vast auditorium, yet Renaissance theatres, when they were designed for opera and ballet, had rarely more than 1,800 seats, and often much fewer. The performances of the strolling players in court ballrooms were small and intimate. But intimacy really became a theatrical element only in the seventeenth and eighteenth centuries, when the spoken word itself became of primary importance. The spoken word in Greek theatre was less important than the ritualistic impact. Its dramatic form is more akin to opera, which is not intimate. How could it be when spoken through masks to ten thousand people?

Since the Renaissance, Western theatre architects have recognized that intimacy is a key factor in the full enjoyment—visual and aural—of drama and opera. In the eighteenth- and nineteenth-century theatre, the economics of the seating arrangements was entirely different. If some of the intimate old theatre interiors were redesigned for a contemporary audience, they would easily lose 25 to 30 percent of their capacity. A nineteenth-century theatre of 2,000 seats would not have sufficient room for 1,500 seats today. Contemporary rules governing safety in public places today require far wider aisles, greater spacing between them, and many more exits. Europe still permits folding aisle seats—a practice unthinkable in America today.

Twentieth-century man is taller and needs greater legroom, as well as better vertical sight lines in relation to the audience in front of him. Also, the ability to hear a theatre performance well was not so much of a problem in previous ages as it is today. Not that earlier designers had much knowledge of how to solve acoustical difficulties; rather, two other conditions helped to solve these problems. First was the style of declamatory speech, which was more audible than the slur and mumble of naturalistic acting as we know it. Actors and singers were taught to project vocally to great distances. Secondly, modern-day traffic sounds and the internal vibrations set up by ventilating and air-conditioning systems seriously cut our ability to understand clearly what is being said onstage. Such noise was less of a problem then than now.

Intimate involvement is important to dramatic theatre today. In a sense, the closeup that the movies have found so useful, we, in the theatre, begin to want. Even early English theatres were intimate in the sense that the audience was packed in, no more than sixty feet from the stage. I do not think that involvement and intimacy are necessarily related. Intimate contact—visual and aural—is the important thing in the legitimate theatre.

The distance that separates actor from audience, however, affects visual and aural perception in different scales. In the fall of 1960, when I was asked to codesign the proposed repertory theatre for Lincoln Center, I decided to make field tests to determine the maximum acceptable distance between performers and the most distant row of the audience. How far can the last rows of seats be and still retain a sense of visual contact with the stage? There is a theory that even in our electronic age when the actor's voice can be amplified, the audience's capacity to see clearly starts to fail first. Although I had already designed a number of theatres, and had for many years been involved in the design of playhouses, I had never actually tested this generally accepted theory. When I say the eye falters, I mean in ability to appreciate the subtle expressions of an actor's face and eyes.

Since facial characteristics and the personal power of projection vary to great degrees, I divided my tests into two general categories: drama and legitimate comedy, and musical theatre. Within each category, I picked out artists whose visual characteristics would cover a wide range. For instance, I studied Julie Harris in James Costigan's *Little Moon of Alban.* This lovely actress has a characteristically small voice, yet her diction and projection carried throughout the entire theatre. Although she could be heard very clearly, I found it impossible to appreciate her expressions and the delicacy of her features from the back of a large house. Then, moving to seats that were fifty to fifty-five feet from the stage, I found that I could fully enjoy her most subtle facial expressions and, naturally, the finer shadings of voice. Miss Harris' performance was of the most subtle character. On the other hand, Gertrude Berg's performance in *A Majority of One* was rather broad comedy. Here, an equally talented and experienced actress was able to project both visually and aurally to the back of a theatre large enough to be used for musicals. When I climbed to the last seat in the second balcony, although the steepness in viewing angle prevented me from seeing Miss Berg's eyes, I was able both to see and hear her clearly. It was apparent to me that while this kind of personal projection was rare in an artist, much of the two actresses' powers of projection was due to the style of direction and the play itself.

For this test I witnessed many other performances, some in the broader style of musical comedy. The broad expressions and gestures, not to mention tremendous vocal projection of an Ethel Merman, can carry to rows over a hundred feet away without too costly a loss of visual enjoyment. Here a completely different scale had to be used, primarily because of the music and movement—dance, breadth of gesture, and style of acting.

The conclusion was obvious: each type of presentation style had its acceptable limits in scale. The scale I found was not an exact one. In general terms, legitimate theatre of high quality, be it drama or comedy, demands intimacy to give the entire audience an appreciation of the aural and visual qualities of a performance. In terms of actual distance, in the legitimate field it is some sixty to seventy feet before a discernible, but decisive, fall-off of visual appreciation appears—again depending on the physical characteristics of the performers. In the musical field, these distances can be extended half again as much.

The owners and those responsible for the financial operations of a theatre are naturally anxious to get as many seats in as possible—either to pay the operating costs, or to lessen the enormous deficit of a subsidized theatre. It is important to keep in mind not only the distance from the stage but, also, the height above the stage. For if a seat is located above the highest architectural member of the stage opening, in the case of a Proscenium theatre, the person sitting in that seat will feel like a secondary citizen. His subconscious instinctive sense of scale is offended, and his sense of contact with the stage is greatly lessened.

Second Balconies

A current controversy concerning the size of theatres, therefore, revolves around the question of including a second balcony. In a past society that accepted class distinction as well as the inevitable levels of economic independence, a multitiered theatre had some justification. But since the patron now shares with the public the responsibility of setting standards, the theatre has become a democratic institution that will not accept class distinction. Anything beyond a single balcony intensifies this nonacceptance, particularly in America. In this country, the attitude is so strong that even in a subsidized theatre, a second balcony seat is the hardest to sell. To a box-office man in a commercial theatre (if not to the producers themselves), it is sometimes impossible to sell second balcony seats—even for a hit production.

I feel that if a single balcony is needed to fulfill a seat quota, then it should be designed in such a way as to make it a more desirable seating area. The comfort and seat spacing must be as attractive as in the orchestra. The approaches to this single balcony must, by their generosity of design, make ticket holders feel this is not a second-rate conventional balcony.

Determining audience capacity and setting up a budget are inseparable factors. The only intelligent way to analyze seating capacity in relation to a budget for a theatre is to see all theatre

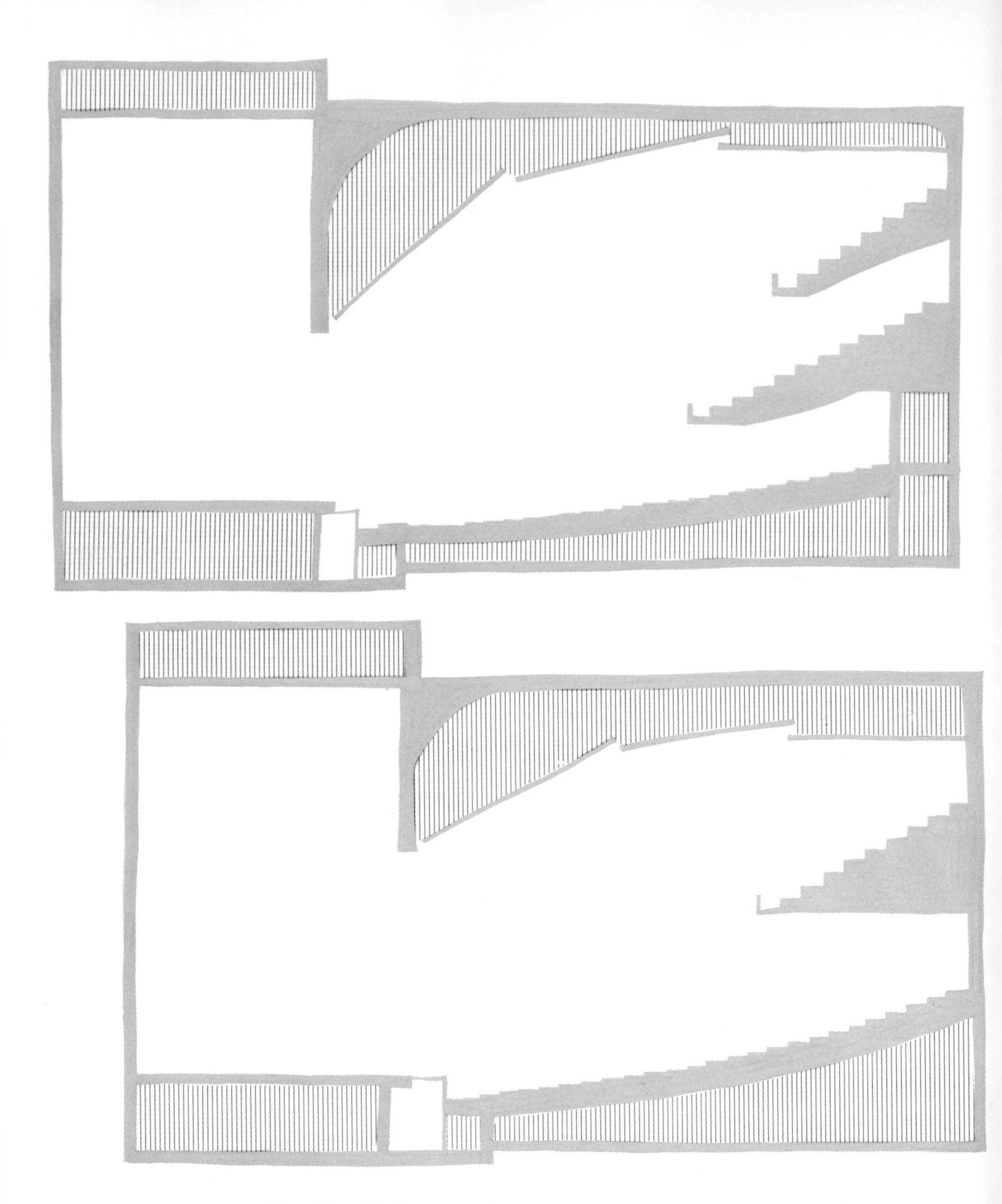

Fig. 41. Today there is a controversy concerning the inclusion of second balconies in theatres. Whereas, second balcony seats engender a feeling of second-class citizenship, single-balcony schemes provide more democratic seating and better sightlines for all.

organizations—regardless of their stage forms—as divided into two basic categories according to administration.

First are the commercial theatres—nonsubsidized organizations that must be self-supporting and must pay an acceptable return on the investment for both the structure and its operations, whether it is the only theatre in a community or one of a dozen theatres in a metropolitan center.

In the second category are the theatres that must survive on subsidy. Included are the regional repertory companies, the community "cultural centers," and the educational theatres in universities and secondary schools.

In the educational theatre, there must be greater stress on intimacy since the student actors do not yet have the experience to project, either with their voices or their acting, to the same distance as trained actors. The students or semiprofessional actors, dancers, and singers who attempt to fill a large auditorium before they have the technical experience to do so can seriously endanger their later development as performers. In the professional theatre, on the other hand, a profitable return on the financial investment can be achieved only when productions play to audiences of large capacity.

Too often, a partially subsidized theatre in an educational institution is planned with the purpose of occasionally housing visiting professional companies. This aim tempts designers and architects to compromise between a capacity large enough for the profitable professional company, yet intimate enough for their own nonprofessional laboratory productions. Such problems of educational institutions are what has led to the ill-fitting multiuse theatres that now abound.

Operating costs also must be considered differently in educational theatres and commercial theatres. Unionized cleaners, porters, and box-office staff are all pertinent to the original programming laid down by the owner in planning a theatre. Organized labor unions have a hard and sometimes restrictive influence on the arts of the theatre in this country.

They are unquestionably right in bargaining collectively for the best wages and working conditions for commercial productions. But nonprofit ballet companies and repertory and opera companies have to meet the same costs for labor that the commercial producer has to meet. This is a major roadblock to true, culturally inspired, nonprofit theatre. Some of the theatre unions and societies covering professional directors, choreographers, designers, and actors are making an effort to give consideration to these nonprofit operations.

Such pressures are mentioned because the design approach to subsidized theatre complexes must realistically accept these restrictive operational costs before a practical program can be completed.

As an example of how these future operational costs can influence design and planning, I cite some of my experiences with Lincoln Center's Beaumont Theater. It was evident to us that future labor conditions would make it imperative that the least amount of manual handling would be essential to achieve a bearable operating cost for the repertory company. I felt also that this situation would affect future lighting crews. In the electrical department, therefore, I designed a system that I call "saturation lighting." The entire area of the stage and forestage has its own prefixed lighting equipment. Each acting area is covered with front light from ceiling ports, a Stage Right and Stage Left light, and a backstage light, each in two colors. When the theatre is changed to its Open-Thrust Stage shape, similar equipment, which is focused on those areas, is merely switched on. The time saved by these flexible systems gives the repertory company additional rehearsal time and also lowers ever-burdensome operating costs. Certainly, however, it added enormously to construction expenses and to the maintenance of the theatre.

Another aspect of operating costs to be considered is when a college theatre decides to sell high-priced tickets for a professional performance, both to students and to the community, it is hard to justify a nonunion labor rate scale. In addition, sophisticated electronic switchboards need trained maintenance personnel, even when there are men capable of doing this who are not members of the electrical unions. This matter also must be gone into as a potential operating cost.

If the tentative decision is to build only one theatre to house both professional and student activities, then the safest course is to determine how small its seating capacity can be. Essentially, this means a rather intimate auditorium, even when the stage house and its facilities are on a large "professional" scale. If 750 seats are thought maximum—this is large for a university theatre —it is better to plan on subsidizing an additional performance or two of a visiting professional production than to pay an additional cost to add another 500 seats that would justify a professional operation. The additional initial cost also increases continuing operational costs since the extra cubic footage needs constant cleaning, heating, cooling, and other maintenance.

In translating these figures in terms of audience capacity for subsidized theatres, nothing is more delightful for a legitimate drama than to have an audience of under 1,000 seats. If it were not for the economic pressures, 700 to 800 seats would be ideal.

In legitimate drama theatres that must be self-supporting, 1,200 to 1,400 seats are about the limit. For opera or musical theatre, one can extend seating capacity from 1,600 to 1,800. Managers or impresarios, however, now say that they cannot make productions pay for themselves without an audience of 5,000 or more.

In determining seating capacity and size of the theatre, such budgetary factors as urban planning, zoning, and real estate must also be considered. The real estate on which it is to be built obviously influences the size of the theatre. What are the taxes? How much of the land can be built on? How expensive is the land? Will it affect the economic setup of the theatre as an investment for the owner?

Another factor is building code regulations and safety codes. In a city like New York, a theatre under 300-seat capacity has an entirely different set of safety regulations, all of which affects the manner of building and the shape of the theatre. In addition, a theatre under 300 seats is classified by the unions involved as an "Off-Broadway" house, and therefore, allowances are made concerning minimum wages and working conditions.

Other considerations are: location in relation to parking and traffic and restaurant availability. How do people get to the theatre? How do they get in and move around? How much parking space is there for cars either directly or indirectly related to the projected theatre? Many cities are passing rules that a theatre building must provide some underground parking. Urban theatres must consider all these matters carefully when determining a budget.

Future owners, board chairmen, finance committees, and donors may establish financial limits and choose sites. Top architects and experienced consultants can and should assist in the creation of the detailed program. But none of them should be allowed to make final judgments. That can be done only by the professional user and operator of the theatre.

Choosing the Theatre Shape

Having determined what size audience they wish to serve, the program should now consider the stage shape their theatre will have. The choice of stage shape is not unalterable. When all budgetary factors and supporting facility requirements are assembled into the program, the architect and theatre consultant may have other suggestions.

As we have seen, there are six basic theatre shapes in current usage in this country. They represent only a few of the many variations and combinations, and ultimately the architect and theatre consultant will best be able to assist the program committee in making the final shape decision.

1. Theatre-in-the-Round or the Arena: the stage is surrounded on all sides by the audience. This arrangement puts the greatest number of the audience in intimate proximity with the performer. Both audience and actor are in the same room, enhancing the intimacy of actor and audience.
2. The Open-Thrust Stage: the stage projects into the audience, which surrounds it on three sides. The entire performing area is open, and no pierced wall separates it from the audience. Both acting area and audience area are in the same room.
3. The Proscenium Stage: a stage that the audience watches through the picture frame of the Proscenium arch. Audience and actor are, in effect, housed in different rooms. This is not an intimate actor-audience relationship unless the auditorium is small in capacity.
4. The Multiform Stage: a stage that either mechanically or manually changes the relationships of the audience and the performers, making use of any or all combinations of Thrust, Proscenium, or Arena Stage.
5. The Multi-Use Auditorium: by mechanical means this auditorium changes its spatial volume to accommodate greater and lesser audiences for large-scale and intimate performances, and allows for the different acoustical demands of drama, musical comedy, concerts, and opera.
6. The Uncommitted Area: this is a flexible association of audience and performers which may assume conventional as well as nonconventional actor-audience relationships.

Supporting Facilities and Areas

Each stage shape will make its own spatial demands for scenery storage. Nonetheless, there are general factors that can be taken into consideration by the building committee. The program must outline, independently of the decision concerning stage shape, what part of the stage can be used for storage of scenery, other than the actual playing area. If a house is to be used for musical productions, it is obvious that there must be some offstage area for bulk scenery platforms and flats that may not fly in the stage fly loft. If the theatre is built with too little offstage room, it may preclude the booking of touring companies and multiscened musicals. It is a question of comparing the cost of additional stage space with the potential income for the owner of the theatre. In the programming it is imperative to decide what is the maximum number of productions that will be stored "live" in the theatre at one time. By "live" I mean a production that can be put on the stage for a performance within a few hours. In the Lincoln Center Beaumont Theater, a large backstage area was designed not for unusually large productions, but rather for the storage of scenery in live repertory during each season. The stage is enormous. We felt that there should bc sufficient "live" storage onstage for as many as five productions at onc timc. This is based on the demands of a repertory playing both modern and classical plays. This aspect of the design has never really been tested, and until such time as five productions are in fact, stored live, we will not know whether the decision to provide such generous stage space was wise. Dead storage is another matter, which will be discussed later.

There are a number of areas where scenery may be stored when it constitutes part of a whole production and must be moved rapidly into position at a precise moment. There are four areas on the same general level as the stage itself: upstage behind the playing area; two areas offstage Right and Left; and directly under the playing areas, though this necessitates a large, rapidly moving lift. For modern, multiscene, rapid changes in most theatres, full stage elevators are impractical and not recommended (because of the dangers when open). Finally there is the area above the stage known as the fly loft. Any theatre that omits this latter space is ignoring the most rapid and quietest method of changing scenery. It can fly scenery at the precise moment of a scene's ending, without even waiting for actors to clear.

Certainly some offstage areas are essential for platforms and other three-dimensional scenery to be rapidly parked. To have an additional upstage area is very important for a repertory company. Omitting an area for flying scenery will severely limit the program of operations. Because the stage house may have the most dominant influence on the exterior, many owners and architects are the first to champion such a plan. One may hear the comment, "A tall stage house will dominate the entire campus!" So does the church steeple. The stage house similarly proclaims openly, "This is really a theatre structure."

The often accepted, truncated stage fly lofts are a poor substitute. Half the height of the practical stage house, they use inferior means, like double-purchase counterweights, to fly scenery. They do not really work rapidly enough for modern, open scenery changes, and are not worth the construction funds that go into them. Better to lay foundations for a good stage tower, to be built when funds are available, than to pretend with halfway measures or to totally ignore a basic technical need.

If a cyclorama is to be included, there must be room to fly it and still use normal scenery and to fly drops below the bottom of the cyclorama. This would mean a fly loft anywhere from eighty-five to one hundred feet high. Although many productions are done without a cyclorama to back up exterior scenery, a repertory theatre will find one essential. Stage wagons, which move on and off, up and down stage, either manually on casters or on motorized tracks, are one of the best ways of handling stage bulk and weight. Where expensive union labor is involved, investment in motors controlled by a chief electrician is a necessity.

Another mechanical aid to be considered is an annular ring. As I use the term, an annular ring is a new type of turntable, devised in my studio, to cut the cost of a turntable but retain all its advantages. It may be described as a rotating doughnut, eight to ten feet wide, set into the stage floor. The circular part of the stage inside the ring remains stable, while the ring itself rotates by motorized controls or on casters under the stage by a hand winch. The prime use of the ring is to bring on or take off scenery; to move properties downstage in an open scene change. As the ring turns to strike one scene, the following set of props comes into

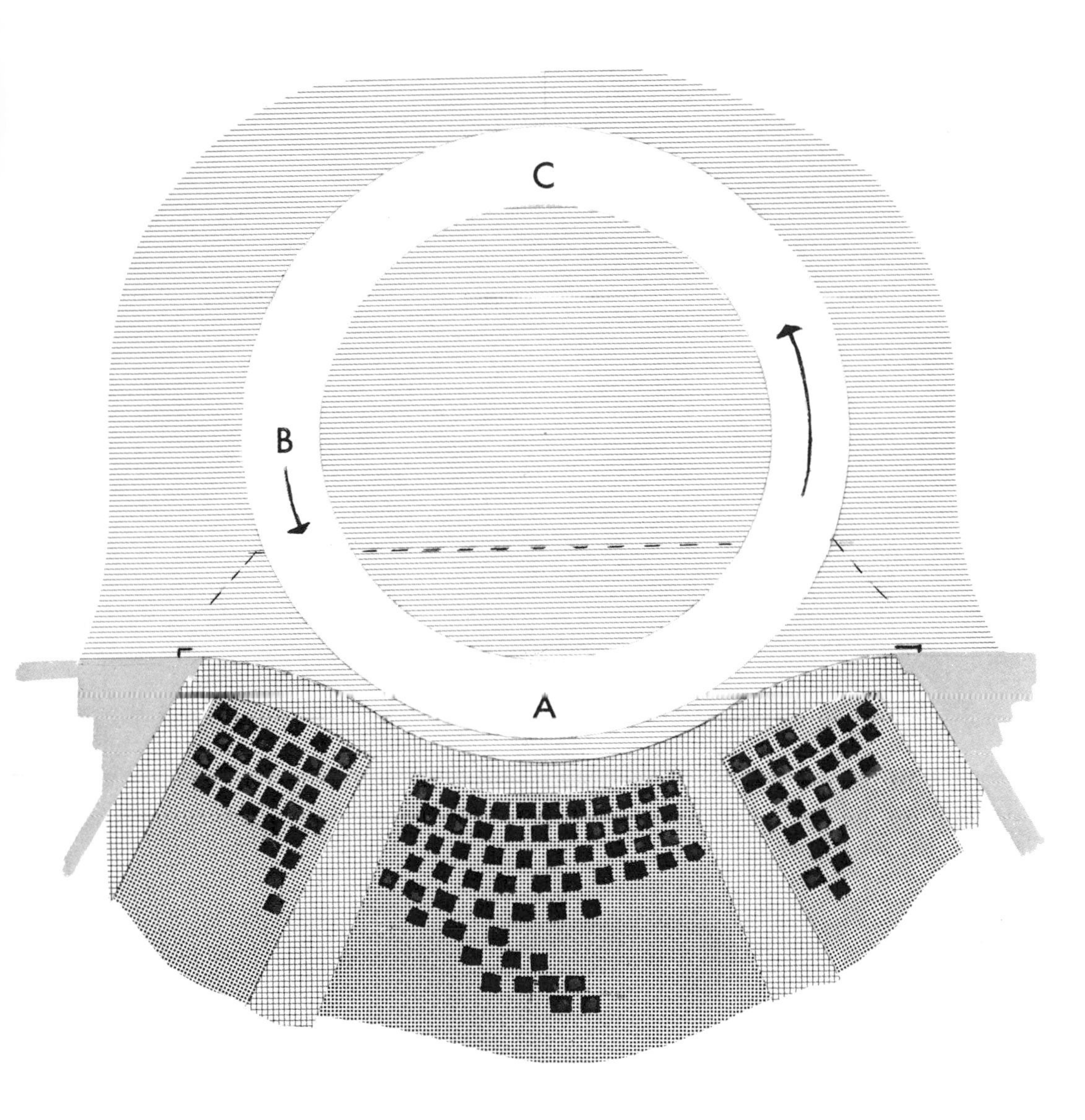

Fig. 42. When the Annular Ring is used for moving properties and scenic elements at the Beaumont Theatre, props onstage indicated at A are rotated offstage to position C. This brings on props for the next scene from position B.

the downstage playing area automatically. As the illustration shows, the annular ring should be placed as close to the downstage edge as possible. When an entire setting is to be turned to the audience (as on the traditional turntable), that set is constructed on a series of concentric casters, which carry the weight of the set center. The outer edges of the "hole" of the doughnut must be movable also. The set is then locked into the annular ring and when both are turned the entire set rotates as one unit. The inclusion and size of turntables, annular rings, and stage traps to permit a repertory theatre to move many scenes rapidly can be ascertained only after a thorough program has been agreed upon by the future users.

Supporting areas of the theatre—for administration, performers, and audience—must be listed with careful questioning to avoid the possibility of overlooking the obvious. In the history of theatre building, there are stories about construction being completed before it was discovered that toilets had not been provided for the audience, or that a box office or dressing rooms for the performers were inadequate or had been forgotten, as we have described earlier.

The functions of a theatre lobby or vestibule are far more important and complex than those of ordinary buildings where basic needs are mainly to keep out weather and reduce the level of street noise. The lobby is a place of preparation, a place of anticipation. Ideally, a theatre should have a vestibule to take care of the purely functional services normally associated with that area. Here the box offices should be located. Beyond this, through a second set of doorways should be the ideal lobby or lounge—a place where everyone can gather and prepare himself in anticipation of the drama. This should not be just a sound and light trap to seal off the atmosphere of the outer world, but a chamber that in its very physical form and atmosphere heralds the mood of the final chamber of performance. No shred of daylight should ever be allowed to penetrate this room. Our contemporary passion for overscaled and huge picture windows should be limited to the outer vestibules only. No matter how attractive the view may be from the theatre looking outdoors, there should not in any way be a distraction from the mood of the inner narthex of our temple of drama. The very level of lighting in this inner lobby should never be so bright that it competes with the high level on the stage itself.

Final Program Checklist

For audiences, any final program must have considered the following: lobby, lounges, and rest rooms for the balcony and orchestra, coat-checking facilities, refreshment counters, water coolers, telephone booths, fire escapes, adequate exits, standing room, a warning system to call the audience to their seats, a place to administer first aid, and, for the recent expansion in our theatregoing public, elevators and wheelchair access for the aged and the handicapped.

For performers, a program should include as primary items: adequate dressing-room facilities, mirrors, shower and rest rooms, rehearsal and practice rooms, acoustically isolated warm-up rooms for musicians, a Green Room where performers can receive admirers and friends after the performance, also an area to get coffee or food during rehearsals. Few commercial theatres used to provide rehearsal space, though for resident companies, a rehearsal room with an area equivalent to that of the stage is now considered essential. Educational theatres are sometimes designed with the lobby or a room under the stage planned for rehearsals.

In a theatre planned for musicals, a performing area for the musicians cannot be overlooked. There is a famous story of a theatre that produced an opera without having an orchestra pit. This was a classic case of the change in use of a theatre that is frequent on the part of managements. A pit for musical comedies or operettas must be large enough for at least twenty-four to twenty-six musicians.

For theatre administrative personnel, there must be office space and equipment for the permanent staff and for those representing the tenant, such as the traveling company manager and the press agent. They too, of course, need toilets and, in some cases, dressing room facilities. They also need a box office for future attractions, independent of current sales.

For production staff, the program must consider crew areas under the stage, accessible loading facilities for rapid delivery and removal of all production items. There must be some kind of decision made about work and repair shops and equipment for building and painting scenery and about storage space for unused scenery. Most commercial theatres do not include paint bridges and frames, a facility somehow lost in twentieth-century theatres. Most educational theatre people consider it ideal to provide their production departments with easy, if not direct, access to the stage, but most often this is a great luxury and an expensive provision. Noisy mechanical rooms, carpenter shops, and paint shops can be made completely soundproof only with a great additional construction expense involving double walls and floors to isolate locally produced sounds.

When vital items have to be eliminated from a building program for economic reasons, the question of whether the shops should give up the expensive acoustical isolation that was planned is always asked. Will the stage be useless for rehearsals if the noise is great in the shops, or will shop activities have to stop during a performance? If these questions are asked in the beginning, the committee may determine it more economical to build a separate building at a lower cost per square foot and on less expensive land, and to pay for trucking and moving time to store and build scenery there. This separation of shops is not recommended—although the commercial theatre has coped with it for years. When final costs are obtained, it may, however, provide significant savings.

Equipment

Needless to say, a secondary checklist, which is part of the subsequent design phase, must spell out the detailed requirements of equipment for each of these facilities. In this design phase, consideration must be given to the separate requirements of such technical aspects as acoustics and structural, mechanical, and electrical engineering. The acoustician must ask if the theatre is so large that it must be provided with amplification for the actors' voices. If so, are speakers and cables for the amplification system to be included in the basic scheme or will they be brought in separately, depending on the requirements of individual productions? Many more such details are part of the design phase after the final program is determined.

Part of the program should list desired lighting equipment, rear projection systems, stage machinery, backstage equipment, control boards, and other such technical items. It is good practice for the program committee to divide these equipment schedules into three parts: first, what is absolutely necessary for the theatre to have when it opens; second, what additional equipment will soon be needed, or would be desirable if the budget allowed; and third, the ideal or maximum equipment that would make the plant operate in the most creative and most efficient way. This kind of subdivided listing in the program is another form of the assignment of priorities. If such a listing is not determined in the planning stage, it may have to be done during the design, or construction, stage, even when pressure of time can make decisions concerning deletions quite serious.

Conclusions

In determining the size of the theatre, both the professional and educational organization should be governed by several basic guidelines: first that the all-purpose theatre is impractical and impossible. Second, it is more desirable that two theatres be built to accommodate all the kinds of live performance adequately. One must first house large musical productions and large dramatic spectacles in which scale of gesture, the massing of voices, the movement of choruses, the large production values can be appreciated from a great distance. The second must be designed for intimate drama and intimate comedy; in these theatres, every seat must be within an appreciably close range for the best enjoyment of sight and sound of the performance.

When the financially responsible authorities of a proposed performing arts center protest to their theatre consultant and their architect that they cannot afford to commission two different theatres, what does one answer? Two irrefutable facts must be brought out. The first, that no single theatre structure can bridge the gap between the requirements for spoken drama and for vocal and instrumental performances. Secondly, if financial considerations really do limit construction to only one theatre, by all means it should be in the scale for spoken drama. The reverse will never work—musical requirements will be overscaled for the spoken word. In the very delicate balance of acoustical design elements, it is never totally successful to rely on adjustable segments of ceiling reflectors, side and rear walls. One can enjoy an intimate musical performance on a small scale, but an oversized dramatic house may be a total disaster, particularly in the educational and semiprofessional fields.

Only after all these essential questions are considered by the building program committee will they be in a position to return to the question of what the theatre shape should ultimately be. When those decisions are made and the understanding is spelled out clearly in a final written program, the client-owner of the theatre can go back to the fund-raising and leave the architect and theatre consultant to the design phase.

Only then can all be sure that they are on an agreed, charted course toward shaping their theatre correctly for its intended purposes.

VII

The Program Committee

To assemble the necessary information and knowledge to write a complete and farsighted program successfully, the client-owner must establish a Program Committee. The principal aim of all those on the committee is to see that the program will examine and outline as precisely as possible all the basic objectives of the future theatre.

Composition of the Committee

Most importantly, the development of a program must be in the hands of all the professional users; but a Program Committee should not be large. Representation of management and finance are essential, naturally. If a client's needs are complex, and it seems that too many people must be represented at the upper echelon, a smaller subcommittee might be formed, consisting only of the actual future users and the theatre consultant. In this case, the consultant truly represents the owner because he is the most objective person on the committee. Such a working group would meet only occasionally with the upper-echelon group (which also includes the consultant), to keep an eye on progress and finances.

To ensure that a theatre will serve the users' special purposes, the Program Committee should include the client's director and technical director, the resident scenic and lighting designer, their technical staffs, the department heads (if the theatre is being designed for an educational institution), the house manager, and other actual production staff.

The architect should attend all such meetings. If he is willing to spend the months that it may take for a program to develop to maturity, he will know at first hand a great deal more about his client's needs before he begins to design. However, some architects may not want to be in constant attendance at all the working sessions of the Program Committee. Others may prefer to attend only the prime, early meetings when basic policies are determined, and then wait for the small working committee to present its first draft.

There should, therefore, be a professional theatre technician on the committee as consultant, who should have as much familiarity as possible with architecture in order to prevent the final program from being too far removed from the facts of architecture (in case the architect should be absent from any of the meetings). This technical adviser could be someone on the staff of the architect, or he could be retained directly by the owner-client. (On the whole, I believe, it is better if this consultant is retained by the owner.) I have been in both situations, and have found that if the consultant is retained by the architect it is easy for the architect to overrule his consultants, where technical function is paramount. The architect can unconsciously, as well as intentionally, withhold information of major importance offered by the consultant. If the consultant is retained by the owner, the latter will at least have the benefit of all the information.

In many instances, there has been no well-rounded technical adviser on the program committee. Rather, the architect or client brings in, at a later design stage, a number of individuals, each familiar with a single element of the theatre—seating layouts, sight lines, or lighting. As we shall shortly see, there is a dangerous tendency on the part of these specialists to see the total problem only in terms of their particular areas. By the very nature of his situation, the specialist is bound to feel some sense of failure if he has not achieved the best and most imaginative layout of equipment and controls that his specialized knowledge and experience can produce.

Better, more consistent results are assured if there is at least one architecturally and theatrically oriented member of the committee at all times, one who can talk in expert terms about architecture and the needs of the director and actors. Such a consultant to the Program Committee can see to it that at the earliest meeting, which must deal with the relative importance of every area, all these relationships are weighed, not only in terms of square footage requirements, but also in relation to the overall operation.

Choosing the Consultant

Unfortunately, there are few knowledgeable theatre technicians who can work closely with future owners and users of theatres in preparing programs. Some directors are strong both in their visual and spatial senses, and in planning and engineering knowledge about this job. There are some architects with first-hand knowledge of theatre operations, who can function as the overall theatre consultant. But even these exceptional men must be given much more than the usual vague outline by a Program Committee. It must be remembered, in designing for a commercial theatre, that once the owners decide whether it will be a theatre for dramatic or musical productions, the physical scale and technical facilities are dictated by the consultant's professional knowledge of contemporary production practices.

How do the client and the architect judge the comparative values of one consultant over another? Finding such experts is like finding a specialist in medicine or any other field—by investigation on the basis of experienced recommendation. The process of the dramatist's and producer's choice of a director for a proposed production is as follows: Candidate X is well known for inventive and very expert handling of the physical movements of actors in and out of scenes; Candidate Y, on the other hand, is known to be very successful in bringing out the best sensitive qualities of their proposed stars. Both candidates are, in a way, specialists. Both tend to stress one phase of their job over the total aims of the production. The playwright and producer choose, therefore, Mr. Z, because his wide experience covers all the phases of the stage director's job. He will not overaccent movement, nor will he become so engrossed with bringing out the star's personal and emotional qualities as to forget that "the play is the thing." These are the attitudes toward potential consultants that clients must assume.

Aside from the normal assessment of man's background, his working habits, his personality, it must be remembered that, in the theatre, questions cannot always be settled on a purely technical basis. Decisions on sight lines are not governed by the formulas of slide rules. Questions on stage lighting positions and angles in various parts of the auditorium are not answered solely by technical manuals. Even backstage, intelligent final judgment on various mechanical means of handling scenic elements, if left to a single specialist, may prove to be a worry when the total theatre starts to operate.

Although one needs certain specialists, such as the acoustician and the mechanical engineer, a team made up of too many specialists may well produce a dangerous situation where their advice comes into conflict with that of one or more other specialists. As an example, an expert on theatre lighting may collide with both the acoustician and the mechanical engineer when they all meet in one area of the ceiling plan where the reflective form, lighting equipment, and the ventilating ducts of the auditorium all "must" be in the same area. Although criteria for a theatre building and much theatre equipment may fall into the pragmatic category of an exact science, many decisions in designing the interior of a theatre—sight lines, acoustics, lighting levels, for example—are not based on exact science, but are subtle matters of relative judgment. There is no such thing as a completely factual solution for sight lines. It is not a matter of the opinion of a single specialist; it can only be a judgment by someone steeped in overall theatre experience—and of someone experienced in the type of production that a particular theatre is designed to house.

Lighting also is a relative element. There is no scientific graph to determine how much light one should have on his program or how much light must be on an actor's face to make it visible from the twentieth row. All these are relative to the comparative light values above or behind the object observed. One sees not by the amount of light, but by the relative value of surrounding illumination. For example, when our eyes are adjusted, we can read by candlelight, but turn on a chandelier in that same room and candlelight becomes inadequate. A lighting engineer in a television studio may justifiably walk around with a light meter, but in dealing with the living theatre, a light meter is of no overall value (unless one needs to test the relative light output of two spotlights from a given distance). A light meter registers only the actual intensity of light and does not evaluate these relative values. As a creative designer, who always lights his own projects, I challenge lighting engineers to produce charts and formulas that can give intelligent answers to comparative lighting levels in the live theatre.

Similarly, although the judgment of an interior decorator could be valuable in the theatre, his commitment to the decor could be as prejudiced as that of the lighting specialist. An interior decorator inexperienced in theatre might feel that the appearance and color of wall coverings, carpets, and curtains should be judged on how they look at intermission time. The theatre man, however, must weigh this in terms of how those decorative items will look when the house lights are out and only the ambient light from the stage affects those furnishings. Nor is the stage curtain chosen solely for its decorative value, but rather for how it will look when the lights go out. The afterglow may be too bright. The reflection of the exit signs may make it seem competitive when the curtain is halfway up, when light playing on it may make it competitive with the stage picture itself.

In the area of theatre administration, also, even the most practiced theatre manager cannot easily judge whether a seat is saleable or not, on the basis of standard economic or box office terms of "front and center." The seat that is partially to one side can be acceptable in a musical theatre where bright music, beautiful dancing girls, and large-scale movement are the important features. But in another theatre where dramatic productions are to be produced, the same far-removed and distant seat may not be acceptable.

Each specialist can give sound advice on these individual aspects of theatre design. But the architect needs another type of expert to deal with the overall theatrical balance. He needs, in the final analysis, the kind of judgment that comes only from long experience and knowledge of the problems of scene design and stage directions—from a direct involvement with all aspects of what actually happens on the stage. It would be wise if the chief consultant is a theatre man with an all-round knowledge—not a specialist in one department. Especially when the architect is faced with drastic cuts in budget, he must have the all-round judgment of a theatre man. What is needed here is the well-balanced compromise, dominated by the knowledge of the whole operation of the theatre, rather than the workings of one part. It is, generally speaking, a director, technical director, or well-rounded scene designer who can best fulfill these overall responsibilities in consultation with a Program Committee.

What Does the Program Committee Do?

Once assembled, the first and primary task of the Program Committee is to write the program. Instead of adding to the expense of the preexecution phase, the committee will, by their competence and foresight, save time and money for the project as a whole.

The Program Committee, with the architect or his representative, should compile a cost estimate of those elements essential to make the proposed theatre function properly. They should exclude all internal items that could possibly be postponed or omitted until additional funds are available.

A well-considered list of priorities must be set up. When faced with balancing the budgetary limitations against the preliminary square footage allocations, the architect can protect the items of high priority and can recommend cutting those of lesser importance without misinterpreting the goals or intentions of the Program Committee. The architect might, for example, proceed to work out a basic cost figure by applying the same trimmed-down figures to the architecture and the mechanical elements. The effect is to avoid the common occurrence of omitting, in the final budget cuts, any items that are essential to the successful operation of the theatre.

Since theatre buildings are usually expensive buildings to construct and equip, a Program Committee should resolve, early in the planning stage, to avoid external or internal adornments—opulent building materials or decorative artworks—until a total listing and cost runoff of all essential structural elements and technical equipment has been determined, unless, of course, financial considerations are no object. Seldom, however, even at such metropolitan complexes as New York's Lincoln Center, are finances adequate to provide the superlative internal equipment necessary for progressive theatre productions as well as luxurious exterior facings. In recent years, any number of ambitious new theatres have been faced externally with imported building materials, while vital technical operating equipment had to be omitted for budgetary reasons.

The ANTA–Washington Square Theatre in New York is an example of a theatre that could well have enjoyed the good taste and style of an architect's contribution, but since the budget was very small, those essential physical elements that made the theatre work successfully had to be housed in a totally unprepossessing prefabricated factory housing. When Robert Whitehead and Elia Kazan were waiting the two-year period of construction before the already existing Lincoln Center Repertory Company occupied the Beaumont Theater, they asked me to donate my time and ideas, working directly with a general contractor to design a temporary structure in which they could rehearse and produce plays.

New York University generously offered free space on one of the empty lots at their Washington Square campus. Since we could afford neither an architectural fee nor the services of an acoustical engineer, I had six months to design and put up a 1,200-seat theatre for a professional repertory company. We quickly decided that we could not afford certain decorative, and even some useful elements. Since this was only a temporary theatre, a stage house was omitted. It was essential to create an Open-Thrust Stage similar to the one that the completed Beaumont would have. Also, we had to have a seating arrangement similar to the actor-audience relationship of the permanent theatre. Nor could we afford a fully soundproof structure. Fortunately, only twice in two years did a performance have to stop during a heavy downpour with lightning and thunder. (Naturally, the audience responded with generosity and interest, and we picked up the action of the play once the noise level was reduced.) We had neither enough space for adequate lobbies or lounges, nor enough toilet rooms, but as a theatre it worked. The audience was enthusiastic; the design was vigorous and simple; and it was achieved by using stock prefab factory materials. The only things made to order were the screens for the stage and the designs of the seating and stage arrangements. The total cost was some $550,000, but it was still incredibly inexpensive.

For a permanent theatre with similarly insufficient funds to execute the ideal, we would have had to spend more for basic things. Vomitory entrances from the stage and excavation under the stage would, I think, be essential. The walls and the foundation of the backstage would have to be built strongly enough so that a stage house could eventually be completed when funds became available. The lobby space would be allotted, even if it wasn't built. The seating spacing would be slightly greater, and even if secondhand motion picture theatre seats were used as at the ANTA–Washington Square Theatre, a more comfortable and better-looking chair could be added when time and funds allowed.

The Program Committee should also face labor costs early. Future costs and man-hours worked per week are not dependably

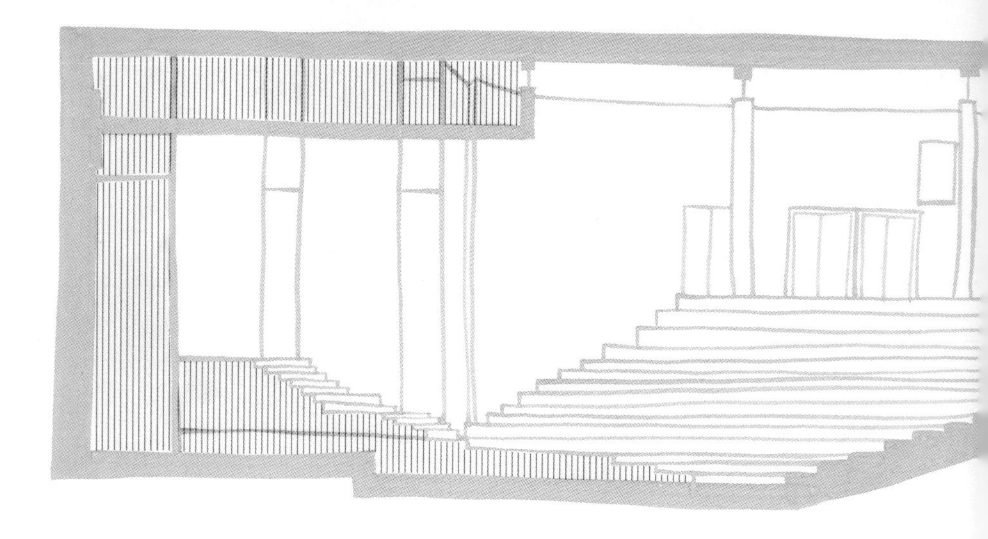

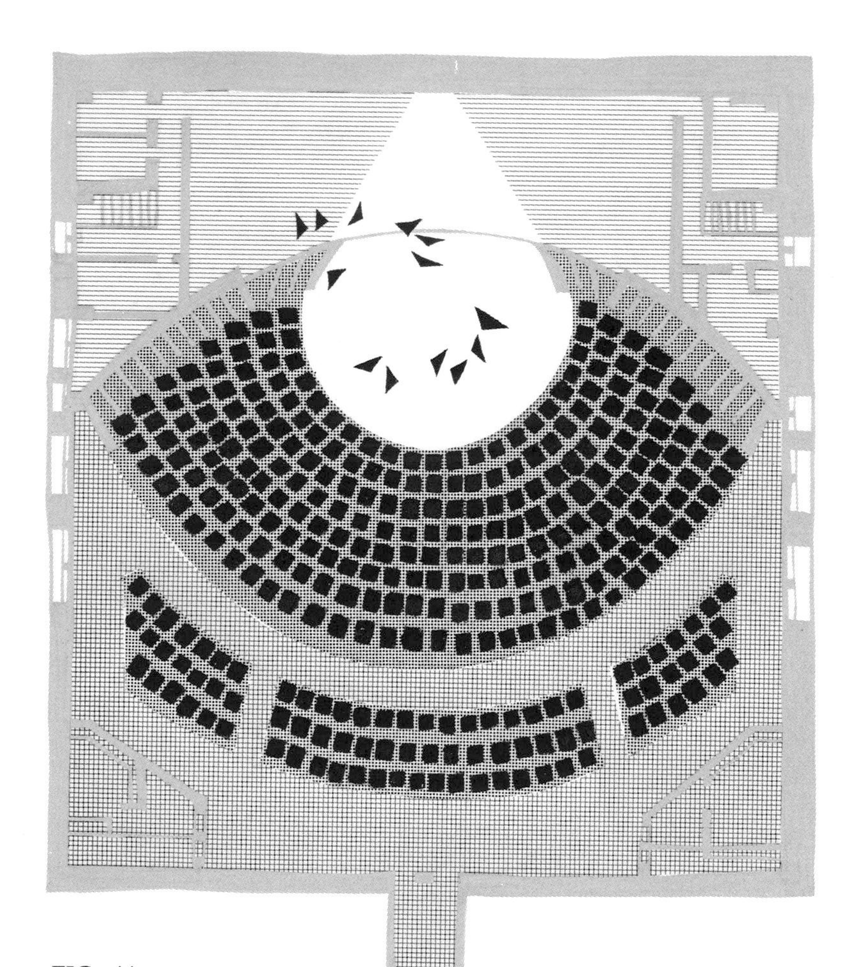

FIG. 44

FIG. 43

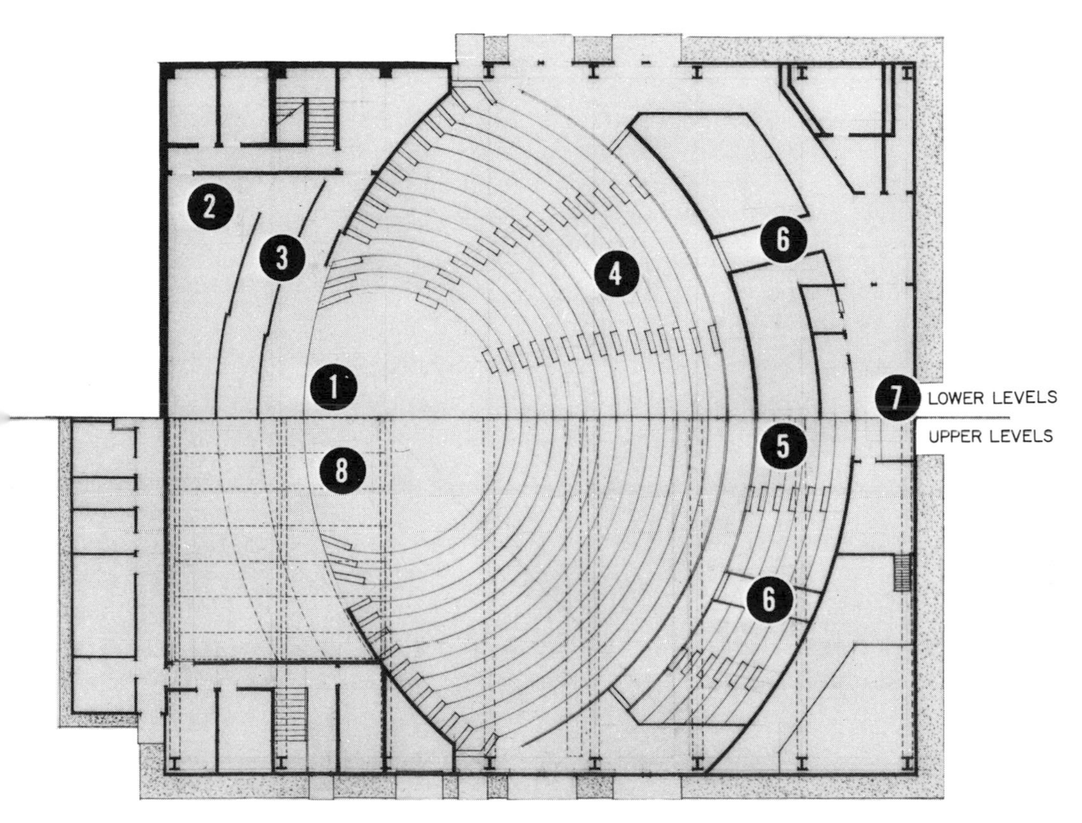

FIG. 45

Figs. 43, 44, 45. The ANTA/Washington Square Theatre in New York provided a temporary and makeshift home for the Lincoln Center Repertory Company before its permanent home was completed. Despite its lack of luxury and comfort it was successful because the relationship between acting area and audience area was clear, distinct, and well thought out.

predictible figures. Part of the preliminary program should therefore deal with time schedules, especially for an educational theatre. Each department head must determine how many hours of the week he believes he will use the stage, rehearsal room, shops, costume room, and so on. There is a desire on the part of everyone associated with a new building to expand the significance of his department in relation to the whole. By determining such a schedule early, the Program Committee can make a more reliable decision about the proposed plant, whether it is large enough and if it has ample working space for all the departments.

With theatre construction costs so high today, another advantage of careful Program Committee study is that the length of time spent in preliminary programming is an investment in cutting overall costs. This preliminary period can run from six months to a year or more, although I have seen it shortened to a matter of a few weeks of intensive work by a team that is expert and can speak with authority for the eventual users.

I was called to a big meeting at a Midwestern university by the architect, Gyo Obata, with all heads of the departments interested in a new theatre facility. After the secretary read a six-page program, I spoke up to say that their program was not thorough. It left too much to the knowledge of the consultant and the architect, and put them in the position of making decisions that might not be a precise reflection of the staff's real needs. In conclusion, I asked the president if he would give us so many weeks or months to sit down with the architects and the department heads to work out a program that fixed specific square footage and the requirements of each department. Everybody agreed, and when asked if it could be done in five weeks, I answered that although I could do it in five weeks, I thought that each department head would not have done enough serious work to meet the schedule. We set a three-month schedule; eighteen months later, we were still trying to complete the program. Although the building was delayed eighteen months, that procedure saved a great deal of money by defining and clarifying absolute requirements.

If the owner-user team has a limited budget, it is essential to state initially what it is. Then the architect and general consultant can make their decisions with some realistic guide. In the last analysis, the final decision in these matters is naturally the responsibility of the architect. He bears the legal burden to the client. But unless the Program Committee has thoroughly analyzed all possible future operations, no sound decisions can be made without risk of delays in the timetable and expensive redesigns later on.

The Building Committee in Action

New York City's Lincoln Center for the Performing Arts was designed as a complex to house five separate and independent structures, each one to be dedicated to a special area of the performing arts. The Metropolitan Opera, the New York Philharmonic Hall, and the Library Museum for the Performing Arts, all with many years of operation in their own structures, gave the client (the future operating owner), the architect, and his technical consultants a clear picture of their operations for working out thorough and detailed programs. However, when it came to programming of the theatres destined to house the complex operations of newly conceived organizations, a conflict of timetables arose. In spite of goodwill and desire on the part of the funding, general programming, and building committees, the results are far from being completely successful. The New York State Theater suffered from the long delay in developing a clearly defined program. The final auditorium and the stage facilities hardly lived up to the high standard set for the generously proportioned and beautifully designed festive lobby. The State needed a place to put on large-scale receptions and parties, so there was a unity of purpose in the lobby.

In the case of the Beaumont Theater, everyone—the directors of Lincoln Center, the building committee, and the two specially selected producing directors—worked feverishly to achieve a perfect repertory theatre. But there were basic disagreements about how to prepare a newly founded acting company. The pressure by the parent body of the Lincoln Center complex to go ahead with steel and concrete, not to mention expensive imported travertine, created conflict with the theatre professionals, who knew full well that an acting company is never born on its two feet. It must be nurtured, trained, and then given the opportunity to act before live audiences. Urgent requests to give the new repertory company a few years to overcome growing pains before occupying the completed Beaumont were turned down. In the meantime, despite wonderful cooperation from the future repertory directors, the architect, Eero Saarinen and I, as his codesigner of the auditorium and all stage facilities, were forced to second-guess in creating a definitive building and operating program. Up to the time of this writing, the Lincoln Center Repertory Company has not actually used the Beaumont plant as a true repertory theatre.

Client–Program Committee Mistakes

Emphatically, I must repeat that too often clients have been guilty of a failure to present the architect with a thoroughly analyzed statement concerning their aims and the requirements of the proposed theatre. The architect must have this statement before he can begin to do any intelligent designing. It is to avoid this pitfall that I strongly recommend the inclusion of a knowledgeable theatre consultant on the committee.

Another common mistake is made unknowingly by finance committees. Far too early in the operations, they insist on having a rendering or model of what their building will look like, in order to spur fund-raising. With all the goodwill in the world, an architect who commits himself to an external shape, before the internal workings are thoroughly investigated, faces one of two dangerous courses. Either he will create an exterior shape that will become a Bible-like precedent to which every other element of the design may be forced to yield; or he will create a model or rendering that will have little or no relationship to the final job. The latter course should be encouraged. There is a tendency in all of us—playwright and architect, painter and composer—no matter how expert in our fields, to find the changing of a sketch relatively easy, but the changing of a "finished" work very difficult. Once a work is finally cast, it is not only expensive to change, but the creator also finds himself resistive to changes. I have seen a multimillion-dollar theatre project suffer from just such pressure being put upon the architect. The Mark Taper Forum in the Los Angeles Music Center is an example. The architect produced, on request from his clients, a model of a performing arts center with a circular drama theatre set in a reflecting pool between two larger theatres. When the architect called me in as consultant and presented the circular form, I asked if the clients wanted a Theatre-in-the-Round. He said not necessarily. Obviously, this was a limiting shape. Subsequently all through the planning and design, everyone concerned struggled to fit adequate theatre elements within this predetermined shape. My design was based on the theory that only props, costumes, and lighting, and no conventional scenery would be used. There was therefore no provision for offstage space, no storage space, no flying space.

Unfortunately, since the Mark Taper opened, the stage has, in many cases, been filled with far more physical scenery than was originally planned. Although some of these productions have been successful, this is a misuse of a simple and formalized plan. Had the artist, occupants, and staff sat down with the architect, the owner, and the consultant, and said, "We want this theatre for intimate productions using scenery," both the architect's circular ground plan, as well as what I designed, would have quickly disappeared. As consultant in this case, I failed to follow up the architect's concept to see if the future users were in full agreement with the built-in limitation of a Theatre-in-the-Round. This is another example of lack of communication, lack of planning, and, I think, a waste of funds. For the next decades, artists working in that theatre will be restricted by a prescriptive rendering and a model that really had nothing to do with the theatre, but only with the fund-raising program.

In the field of university theatre design and in the plans for a true repertory theatre, a different problem is apt to arise. In both categories, there are professional artistic and technical directors. They hold responsible positions as the immediate operators of the proposed theatre complex. They and their entire staffs—down to costume designers, property makers, lighting directors, and many others—usually have dogmatic ideas and (even if this had been their one and only theatre experience) some prejudice against forms and equipment unfamiliar to them. In these cases, both the general consultant and the architect should point out objectively and firmly to the chairman of the theatre building committee, or the president or the board of regents, that this proposed theatre building may well outlive the tenure of any and all current members of the theatre staff who will first use the building. This problem only emphasizes the necessity for a strong team of an architect and a theatre consultant whose combined knowledge and reputation can ensure, as far as possible, the long-range view when making basic decisions during the early programming period.

No one can say that there is really only one way to solve the complex coordination between the architect and the committee charged with developing a careful program, an ultimately effective design. From my own experience—working both as a codesigner with architects and also as the client's technical consultant—I offer these personal ideas for guidance in future client-architect relationships.

VIII

Theatre in the Future

When contemplating the shapes of our future theatres, we must ask whether tomorrow's designs will be innovative or traditional. In form, as well as outlook, will they be directly imitative of the past, or free-thinking about the future? The oracle is caught between a veritable Scylla and Charybdis. No vital, truly contemporary theatre can be conceived by traditional knowledge alone; on the other hand, the designer whose sole credo is "innovation" is either dishonest in proclaiming unequivocal divorce from past tradition, or is apt to produce an ill-conceived theatre design—one that when put to the test may fail. For a theatre, unlike a sculpture or painting, must fulfill complex functions. Although certain aspects of a new design may be original and heretofore untried, the overall creation must be based on trial and error by centuries of "innovators."

The Ford Foundation's eight "Ideal Theatre" projects, which were mentioned in Chapter I, all reflected the search for fresh concepts. However, the best of the designs was founded on traditional, professional practice and added a contemporary innovative twist. The few designs that were totally innovative were unworkable then, and will remain so. They were the egocentric expressions of artists who refused to meet the functional needs of actors, directors, or audiences of today or tomorrow. For storage areas, rehearsal space and dressing rooms, instrument storage and warm-up rooms may all be unseen by the audience but they cannot be dismissed by the staff, by performers, or by theatre designers, architects, and consultants. Whim, as I have said, is seldom realized in theatre construction.

Nevertheless, we must bring new thinking into the theatre to overcome present limitations. Besides audience expansion through sight-line design, I would also suggest reexamining theatre management and construction techniques to make the performing arts available to more people. Self-supporting theatres must recognize a startling fact about their current management practices. They are expensive plants, earning income only twenty-four hours a week—eight performances of about three hours' duration. If we change their shapes, perhaps these buildings could double or triple their activities and incomes.

Creative theatre tomorrow must have greater, not less, subsidy. Federal, civic, and state aid must help encourage the best in communication arts in the future. But even if it does, we who can influence theatre shape and technology must use our imaginations to cut the staggering overhead costs and to increase audience capacities and consequently revenue.

Since economic pressures have not yet, by any means, reached their peak, we must, for one thing, find ways to retain intimacy while increasing audience capacity. In our present Proscenium theatres, we have surely reached the limit of audience capacity. They already seat as many as possible within the sixty to eighty-five feet acceptable viewing distance from the stage, and Proscenium theatre seating could not be widened without reducing visibility of a performance in the corners of the rectangular set. But what about future Proscenium theatres? Might there be a design technique of increasing audience capacity in Proscenium theatres without impairing sight lines?

Sight Lines for the Future

Several years ago, I decided to make a study of where the most dominant action has been located on the stage. From the files of some hundreds of productions I have designed, I picked out about fifty that were representative—dramas, comedies, musicals, ballets, and operas. On overlay tracings of the different ground plans, I marked an X on the stage area where the most important scenes were played, the pas de deux danced, or the great numbers sung. Almost all of these productions had been produced in conventional Broadway theatres, where there was usually a shallow apron between the thirty-five to forty-foot Proscenium arch.

When all the ground plans, each with a number of X's, were superimposed on a master plan, the resulting pattern formed a distinct triangle. The triangle started a few feet in from each side of the Proscenium and ran straight across the apron; its apex was

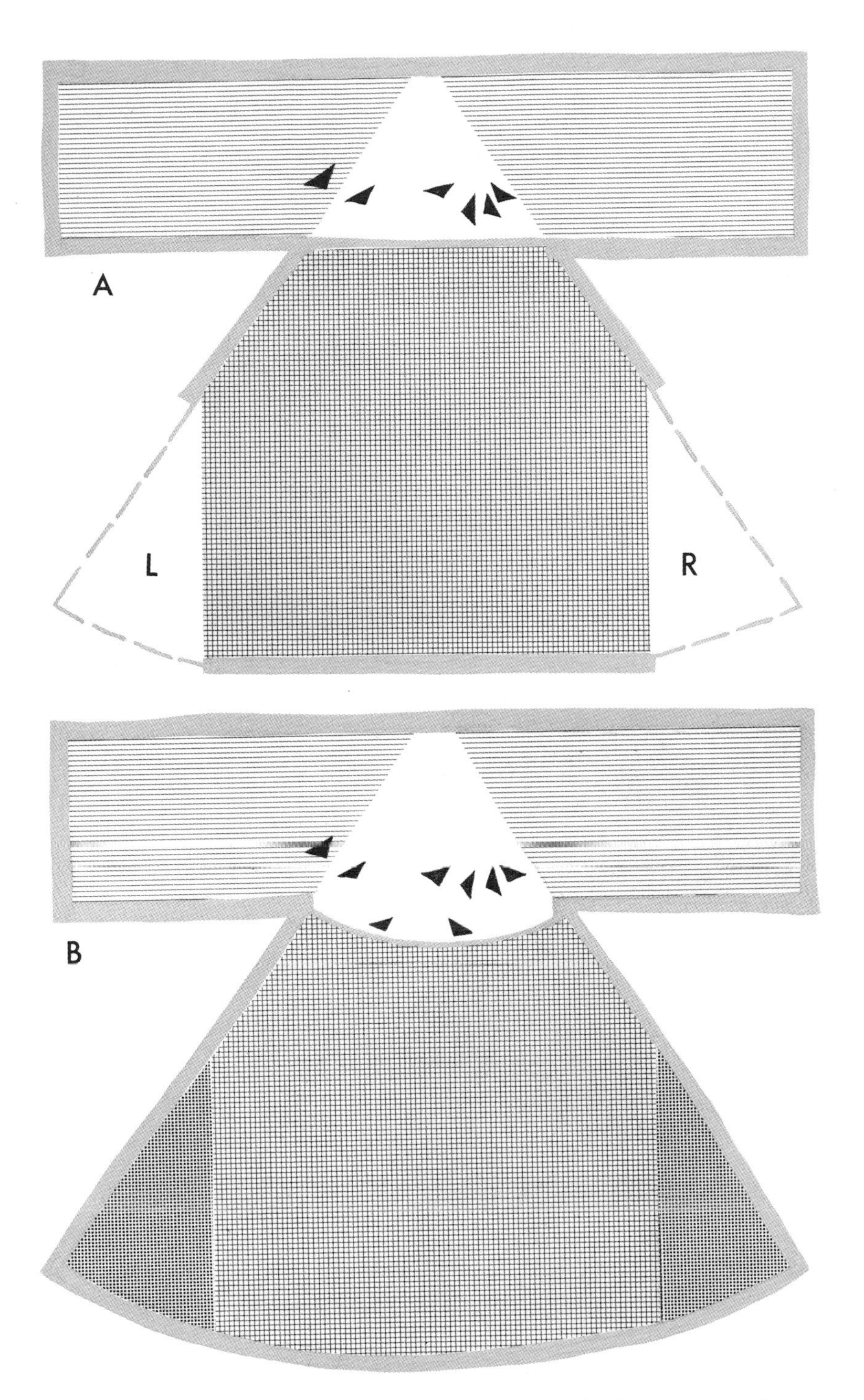

Fig. 46. Additional seating could be included in Proscenium theatres if the audience area were increased on each side to make the plan more fan shaped.

located almost center stage, and not over ten feet back of the setting line, where the pattern of X's was heaviest, downstage and in the center. It was clear that despite naturalistic styles of acting and staging, the instinct of directors and leading actors, singers, and dancers is to get as close to the audience as possible during the high points. At the same time, they wanted to be as near to the center of the stage as possible without obviously "doing a number front and center."

Studying this chart brought me to the realization that I could double the area of that triangular playing pattern. This could be done by bringing back a generous forestage—by extending the center of the stage ten feet beyond the curtain line in a gentle curve from one side of the Proscenium to the other. What this suggests is not new. It is really a development of the ancient tradition of the Open-Thrust Stage. On the proposed forestage (not a real thrust, but a tentative one nevertheless) the scenes could be played close to the audience. Bringing the action forward onto the forestage, the sight line potential to right and left will be expanded, and this will consequently increase potential audience capacity. What I suggest for future Proscenium theatres

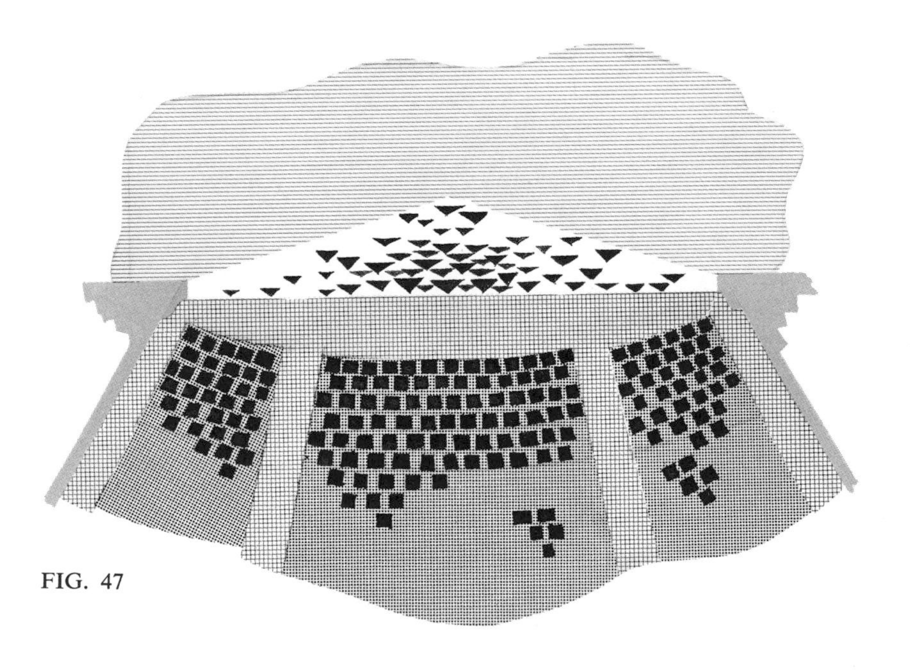

FIG. 47

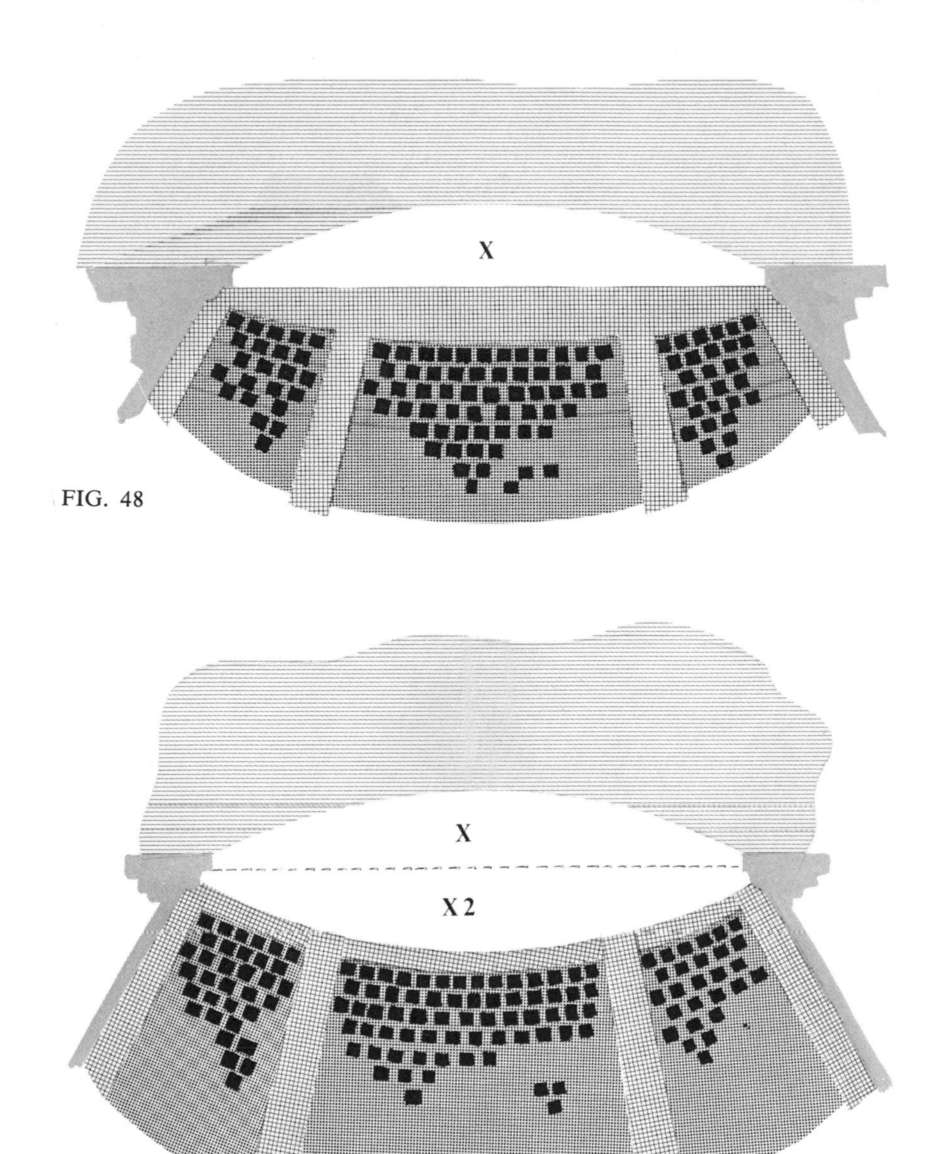

FIG. 48

FIG. 49

Figs. 47, 48, 49. Starting with the area where all major scenes are played, this composes a triangle with its apex upstage (Fig. 47). We can then modify the shape to a curved forestage (Fig. 48). To double this area, the triangle, or modified curve, can be flipped forward as shown (Fig. 49), making a modified Thrust Stage.

then is the addition of a tentative Thrust Stage, with an auditorium in which the side seats slope off a little way and run straight back. By widening the auditorium at the sides of the stage, this solution would permit an increase in audience capacity without putting seats so far back from the stage that they provide only distant vision and permit only a slight sensation of contact with the performers.

To demonstrate how an increase in capacity at the sides of the auditorium would be valid once the rectilinear viewing aspect of the Proscenium staging was altered, I proposed the following formula: If X represents the distance of the farthest seat from the stage, XL represents the acceptable distance of the farthest seat for "legitimate" plays and XM that distance for larger-scale "musicals." By swinging an arc from the apex of the upstage triangle, I found that the number of seats could be increased markedly on the sides, and still provide perfect vision of the performance. Not only would this hold for downstairs, but it would also apply to a balcony of the same shape.

This, then, is a new approach to the design of seating plans for Proscenium theatres. It does away with the ineffective straight seat rows, which are justifiable for films or closed-circuit television, but not for the communal experience of the living theatre. Here, being conscious of one's neighbors is essential to the ritual.

However, with this new approach, we will not be able to retain the old concept of the box set. Rather the designer must work with a parallelogram in mind—similarly a fresh approach. In any case, there are many areas in all sets that are, in a sense, secondary atmospheric background rather than vital playing areas. When, for example, the Lincoln Center's Beaumont Theater is used in its Proscenium form, the area onstage planned for use is in the shape of a triangle—not the shape of a box. When the Proscenium width is forty feet, the depth of the triangle upstage is thirty-two feet (measuring from the face of the apron). When the panels are opened to fifty-eight feet, the triangle extends to forty-seven feet upstage.

This tentative Thrust Stage would, of course, be possible only if the house curtain were relocated so as not to drop on the scenery. Therefore, since this study I have made both the asbestos fire safety curtain and the house act curtain follow the downstage curve of the forestage, as in the Beaumont. This not only allows the curtain to fall on important downstage scenes, but it also enables the designer to put scenic elements on the forestage.

This concept can be of valuable assistance to art theatres, universities, regional theatres, and the professional theatre as well, where the problems of audience capacity are even more serious. True, it will create a new direction and technical problems for production designers; but the approach to sight lines solves many problems for stage directors. The result would create more excitement in the theatre, and would be one means of significantly increasing the number of seats in a house.

In addition, our future theatres could be designed with spaces and versatile equipment to meet the needs, not of a single occupant, but of three or four occupants during the week. Why should there not be both 6:00 P.M. and 9:00 P.M. performances? Why not three more matinees a week of a different production—perhaps for children's theatre? Why not use our theatres on Sunday afternoons and evenings? Industrial shows could be booked in the mornings. To increase the usefulness of our theatres we also must add dining facilities, bars, and much more useful lounge and lobby space.

In terms of future construction, I would propose prefabricated theatres that could be made available in quantities at perhaps one-third the cost of custom-made structures. Two basic models should be investigated. First, a moderate-size, simply designed prefabricated theatre, for which all technical equipment and furnishings—backstage and out front—would be pruned to basic essentials and would also be prefabricated. The second of the two prefabricated theatre designs would be planned for community centers and larger university communications centers—again with the basic structure and all internal components prefabricated. If the mobile home market can build up the kind of prefabricated house industry that it has, then with some government assistance, perhaps the mobile theatre audience could build a proportionate industry.

Satellite Theatres

The free-enterprise theatre suffers from feast or famine. If notices are bad, houses are half full, and high operating costs force the producer to close the show. If the reviews are enthusiastic, the public response encourages a lengthy run. A long-extended success that may bring wealth to producers, authors, and actors brings, at the same time, a secondary, unhealthy reaction. Performers get stale. The entire tempo and creative force that launched the opening begins to fade away. Long runs are detrimental to an artist's development. In a repertory theatre, the constantly changing roles—changes both of character and of relative importance—give freshness to talent and enhancement to development.

Aware of this danger, I proposed, some years ago, a theatre-construction compromise that would avoid the ill effects of an overly long run without loss of profit to the investors—monetary or creative. My idea was based on the unalterable axiom that live intimacy between performer and audience must be preserved—perhaps even improved by smaller, more compact auditoriums—but it also recognized that the theatre might not be able to afford this luxury. How can we increase audience capacities and yet make more intimate live theatre performances more accessible to those who cannot pay for them? How can we do this and yet avoid the debilitating long run that seems to be necessary for financial survival?

My concept—still new and untried—was to go into effect when a new production begins to look like a smash hit, that is, when advance sales or smash reviews after the opening appear to guarantee a long run. I propose that such productions be housed in a complex of theatres—Theatre A and Theatre B. Theatre A would be for live performances; Theatre B would show these performances as relayed by closed-circuit color television.

Theatre A would have a seating capacity of not more than 1,500, if planned for musicals, and not over 850 to 1,000, if planned for drama. All seats would be on the orchestra level. It would be a deluxe, lavishly comfortable, yet intimate auditorium, and would have a number of television cameras in different locations. Theatre B could be a single auditorium, or a complex of two piggybacked auditoriums. Each would have a capacity of 1,500 and a 40-foot closed-circuit television screen. Theatre B need not be adjacent to Theatre A; television cable could connect the two, whether they were next door or separated in a single city or in different metropolitan areas.

With a smash hit, Theatre A would have 12,000 people per week participating in live theatre, with more comfort than presently. If two Theatre Bs were sold during the same week, 24,000 additional people would be able to see the same performances. At the end of six months, over one million people would have

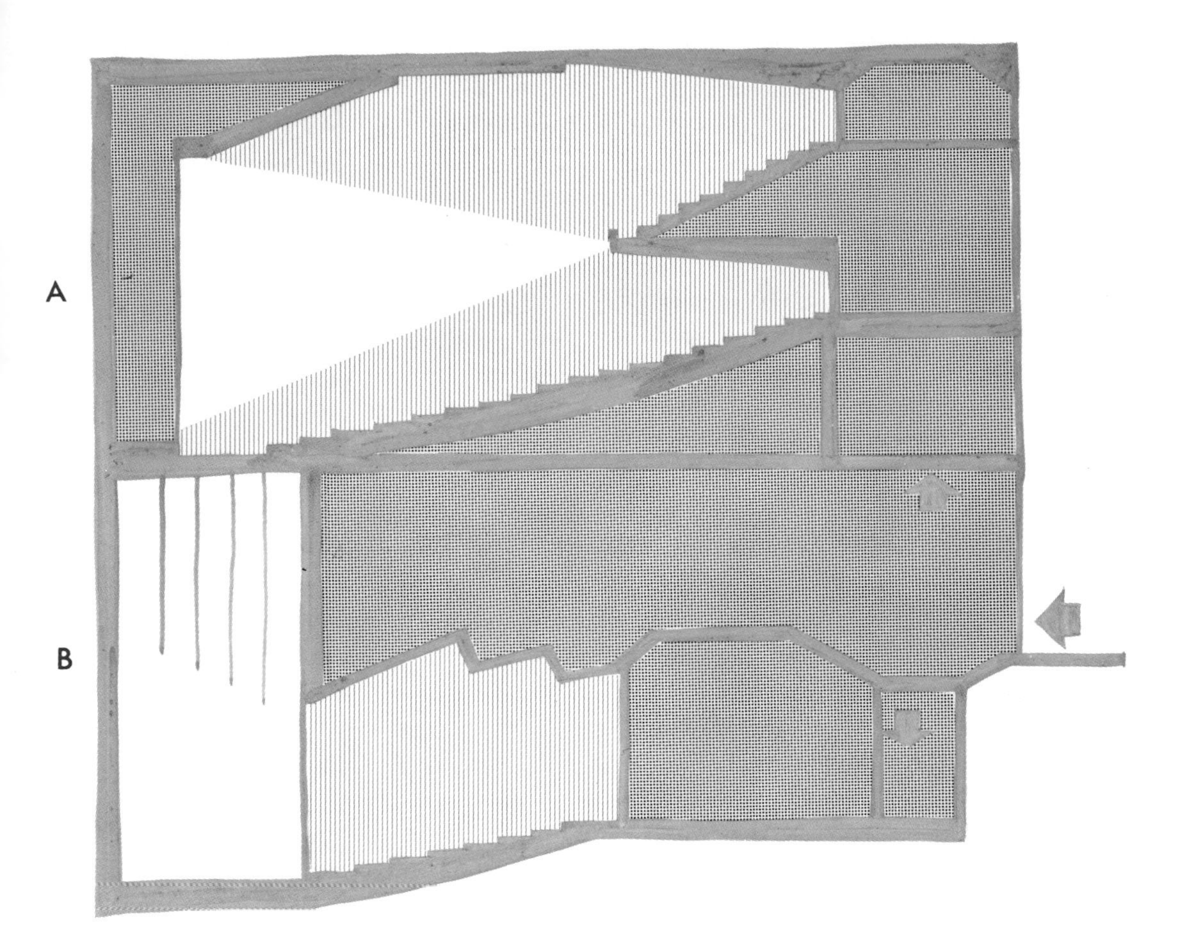

Fig. 50. Combination theatres, one showing live performance, and another showing televised versions of those performances, would extend the audience capacities of today's productions.

seen the play or musical. It now takes almost a year and a half to reach that figure with our current system of single theatres.

This scheme clearly has the advantage of shortening the otherwise long run of a hit play. The entire audience would see fresh new performances, and many artists who are now unwilling to sign for the "run of the play" would be attracted to these shorter runs.

Of course, we must admit the disparity between live drama and closed-circuit television. My feeling is, however, that the knowledgeable theatregoer, who would not think of missing a live performance and who can afford not to do so, will continue to buy tickets for the live performances in theatres of type A. On the other hand, thousands of people do not go to live theatre today, either because of the high cost and difficulty of getting seats or because they get to metropolitan centers only infrequently. Our live theatre is fast losing what for generations has been its backbone—the educated middle class. Rather than miss the play entirely, or wait two years or so until performances may be stale, this audience could attend theatres of type B.

By dealing realistically with these factors of different financial means, distance, and long runs, our theatre might accommodate a new and wider audience. Theatre A could charge even more for the greater luxury of the auditorium and/or the appeal of the live performance in the same space. Tickets to Theatre B could be sold at prices competitive with first-run film houses, or at least at prices lower than the usual balcony-seat ticket. In this way, the income from the condensed run could be the same as in our long-run system.

This concept of hybrid performance offers several secondary advantages. Although only critics and affluent first-nighters could see a live opening night, a production that had shown strength out of town or in previews could open to an increased audience in Theatre B, who would also be able to witness, by television, the arrival of celebrities and the social glamour of opening night. In addition, when no widely attractive productions were available to book into such a network of theatres, theatres of type B could show films or other television programs.

Also, by maintaining the production as a live performance, the rights for future filming would not be jeopardized. A hit that runs for two or three years usually protects itself by delaying the time before a movie of it can be made and released. This concept of the condensed run would also reduce that delay. And finally, with audience acceptance of televised live performances, the enormously increasing expense of touring companies might be cut, and the production be made available to areas that could not otherwise support a live road company.

The shape of auditorium A for live theatre viewing would be controlled by a Proscenium of about thirty-eight feet maximum for a legitimate theatre. The seating plan would be narrower than average, fanning out not over 20 degrees of either side of the center line with no need for deep and high balconies. This interior molded depth would be from 15 to 20 percent less than in the normal theatre interior. This fact alone would contribute to the ability to achieve normal acoustics without the aid of the type of amplification we suffer from today.

Theatre A, for musical productions, could possibly have a wider Proscenium of up to forty-five feet. If a generous forestage were used, the angle of viewing would be greatly extended, possibly farther than in the average musical houses as we know them today.

The closed-circuit Theatre B for live TV would have a shape governed by the size of the giant television screen and the depth and width of a single balcony designed for the maximum comfortable viewing distance. The sound here, of course, would be amplified, and the visual aspect greatly amplified over the living theatre.

Such a concept of electronic relay of live performances will take imaginative management on the part of producers, and innovation on the part of technicians, but it could lead to broadening the base for live theatre and to the education of future audiences.

Electric Scenery

The effect of electricity on the shapes of our theatres can only be enormous, if we project into the future the kind of influence that it has had on the rest of our culture. Three-dimensional scenic elements, achieved with multiple film projections shown simultaneously, must have great influence in times to come. The potentials of projected scenery have not been fully realized in the theatre.

Yet modern visual media are part of every man's daily life. Sensory perception has been expanded to a degree never before attained. Black-and-white and color films, television, and even magazines and books are designed to be looked at rather than read. Peripheral visual impact and subliminal audio influence, which have proved effective in advertising, should surely become a part of our new theatre vocabulary. These potent means must influence any artist with plans for improving the shapes of tomorrow's theatre—at the very least in planning for simple, front-projected and rear-projected scenery.

Unfortunately, we are all still hanging on to the conventional box set and literal realism. Man's fascination with the illusion of depth is much more than a flirtation with the art of pinpoint perspective. Realism is still a dominant trend today because many playwrights, and even stage directors, tend to adhere to the false theory that truth, or veracity, is best supported visually by literal realism. These concepts should have little effect in contemporary theatre since television, still photography, and motion pictures are capable of creating realism much more convincingly.

My objection to literal realism does not mean that in certain types of playwriting selective realism is not valid. Selective realism stresses certain expressive elements of a setting while essential details are either omitted or reduced to the simplest suggestion. A modern version of an Ibsen play might well be designed in this manner. There would be no loss of a period sense—in fact the character of the 1880s might be even more beguiling by being selective.

The more we suggest in the simplest and most provocative ways, the truer we will be to the medium. Generally noncritical audiences are intrigued by the effects of trompe l'oeil, and even by a totally executed, realistic setting, but they are quick to accept imaginative and symbolic solutions if they are boldly and clearly conceived.

When I used leaf projections in *Death of a Salesman* to suggest the passing of the seasons, audiences easily accepted this symbolic image of time passing. I have found that timidity is not so prevalent in audiences as it is in authors, directors, and producers. Most designers worth their salt are eager and able to use this approach—they are all convinced that literal realism is the least creative of all approaches to the visual style of living theatre. It may be dangerous and dogmatic to prophesy tomorrow's theatre trends, but I can say safely that the purely illusionary approach of the past has little to contribute to tomorrow.

As we know today, multiple films are expensive and time-consuming. In productions like *Laterna Magika,* the Czechs have done extraordinary things with films to imply three-dimensional elements. But since their experiments are totally subsidized by the Czech government, they think nothing of expending the time of large staffs, and equally large amounts of money for development. Neither the wealthiest commercial producer nor the most subsidized theatre in America can begin to have a comparable research budget. Yet projected, three-dimensional images must come within our means. I think it is the true approach for theatre today—even more so for theatre of the future. The possibilities are enormous, as is the potential effect on theatre shape.

Electric Lobby

The future may also extend the electric scenery effects to the rest of the theatre. A lobby and the auditorium will no longer be reflections of the European palaces or of the ghastly frauds that were perpetrated in motion picture palaces. Audiences tomorrow should no longer have to face comparatively meaningless decoration—crystal chandeliers, lush fabrics—while awaiting the moment of theatrical truth.

The theatre interior might wear a number of costumes itself. For an evening of tragic drama, it might have one aspect, and for a play of gaiety and glamour, an entirely different one. As we leave the outside world and enter the lobby, we should be immediately drenched in a new atmosphere—one that reflects the world we will enter in the auditorium. During intermission, as well as before the performance, an audience can be steeped in visual and aural material that extends the stage performance. Similarly, architects' exterior designs may reflect this extension of the dramatic experience. We should not stress the seat in which one is an observer, but the overall place where one is a participant.

In the world of the theatre, where we are dealing with a man's dreams, we leave the laws that govern the outer world behind. The dramatist, actors, scene designer, director, and technicians work in an atmosphere that denies the laws that control us on the outside. These magicians of the theatre do not swear to tell the truth, the whole truth, and nothing but the truth. They take a different oath. They put their hands on the Book of the Muses and swear to tell only the truth as they see it—without being dull or boring. And they swear to omit every part of the truth that is insignificant to their dramatic context.

In addition, the measure of time in the world of the theatre is unrelated to the everyday clock we live by. In the period of a two-hour performance, a dramatist can compress a man's entire life-span. In a twenty-minute scene, he can dramatize a few significant moments in a human being's life. The laws that govern light and dark in the outside world are denied here. The shadows are man-made. The sun and moon of the theatre are conceived and created by man. Even color has no direct relationship to the outer world. Three-dimensional form is a snare and a delusion. No sound of the outer world is allowed to enter here. All we see and hear is mastered by the magicians of the theatre. Space itself is controlled. From the infinite to the most intimate it is all pure theatre, pure theatrical reality in a world of its own.

This means that the shapes of our theatres will continually be changed by the most inventive of changers—man's imagination. Electrical amplification of the actor's voice is imperfect in its application and is rejected by many selective artists now, but someday it may permit theatre shapes and sizes to change, limited only by the viewing ability of the spectator. Yet tomorrow, who knows? Some amplification of vision may be developed that will allow some types of theatres to extend beyond our current acceptable depth.

Serious proponents of theatre arts look with grave doubts on the day when mechanical means may dominate the style of production. The solutions to creative theatre of high quality must inevitably embrace the live intimacy of drama. New media of communication may outstrip the films and television of today. But the theatre we are discussing—in visible interior and physical dimensions—must also enjoy inner, creative expansion.

Projects

Figs. 51, 52, 53. For a theatre in the round, I propose adding two elements that can give a lift to theatres devoid of conventional scenic pieces. First we can project scenic images either abstract or semirealistic on both the ceiling over the acting area, and over the entire audience area. Ten projection instruments could cover the entire dome with multiple or overlapping images.

Second, the stage could have lifts (Fig. 52) which could vary the playing area in height as well as provide a means of changing scenic elements. Roller pallets could rapidly re-dress the lift tops, either singly or as a pair. The neutral area at the center of the stage would serve as a "refuge" for an actor who remains on stage while the lifts are lowered.

Four tunnels or vomitories provide entrances for actors and props; smaller aisles are solely for audience.

Figs. 54, 55, 56. In this age of complex technology some machinery is unavoidable. Although on the whole, in the free-enterprise theatre, far too much attention is given to this mechanized approach, any device that can cut down the strangling operating costs of scene changes is justified. In educational and community theatre, however, I recommend the avoidance of this approach.

To answer a university's request for a simple experimental design for use by students, I have designed a circular or "ring" theatre. Basically, it has a small circular interior with a grid from which lighting instruments may be hung in any position. Safe catwalks above the grid permit students to operate this lighting equipment conveniently. For audience seating, four sets of bleachers are set on guide tracks. Overscale wheels permit each of the four sections of bleachers to be moved around the room at will. Access to each scene unit is by the aisles of each section.

The theatre can be arranged as a center stage with four entrances between the units (Fig. 54). The seating could be rolled around to produce an Open-Thrust arrangement (Fig. 55). The seating units can also be arranged as two separate units facing each other. This simple theatre should not be thought of in terms of large capacity. It should hold a maximum of 100 to 200 seats. However, to expand the scale of this scheme a circular balcony could be added at the perimeter. Supporting elements such as dressing room, props and costume shops, and the lobbies and box offices should be in the four corners of a rectangular structure housing this round interior theatre.

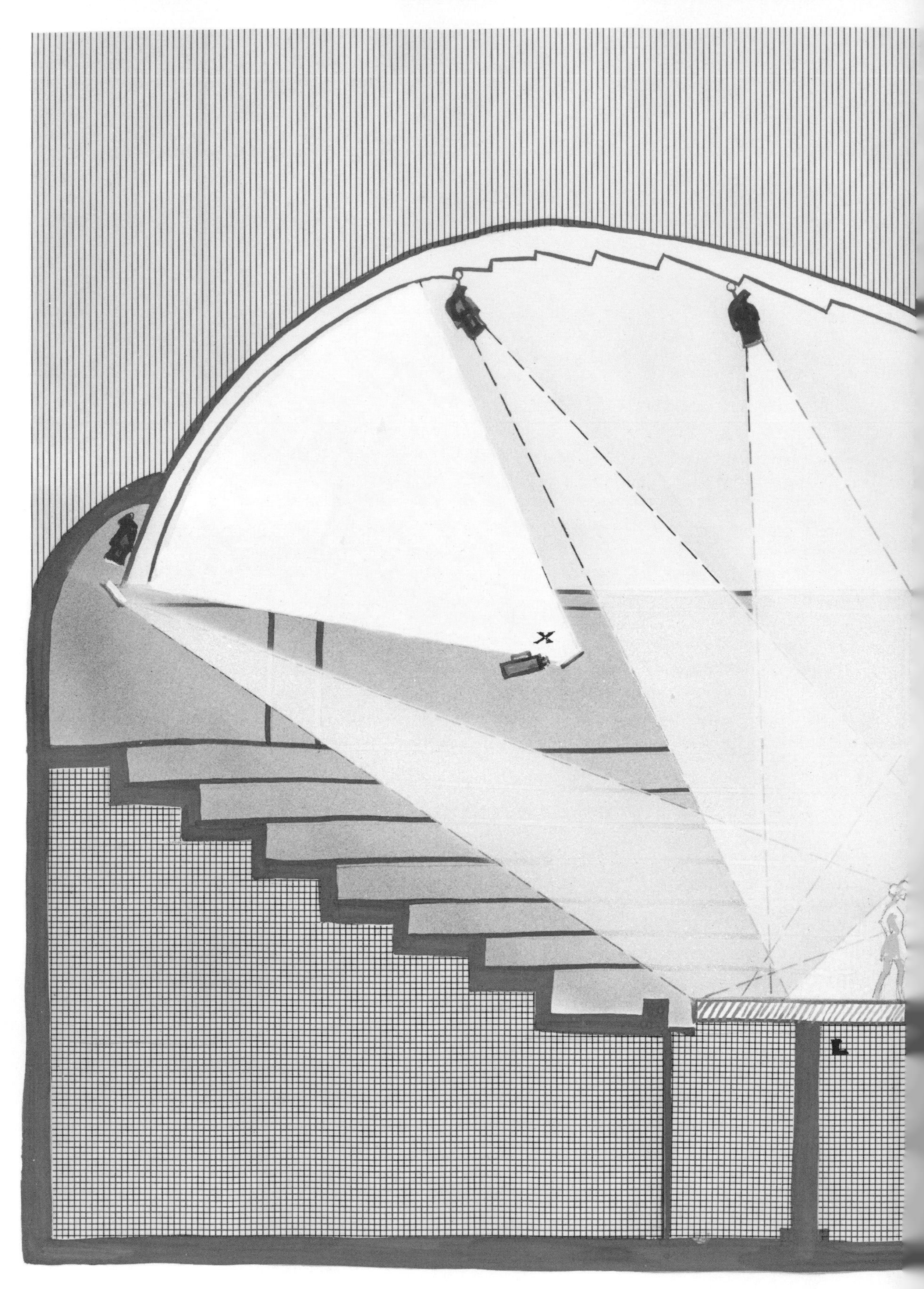

FIG. 51

X
L

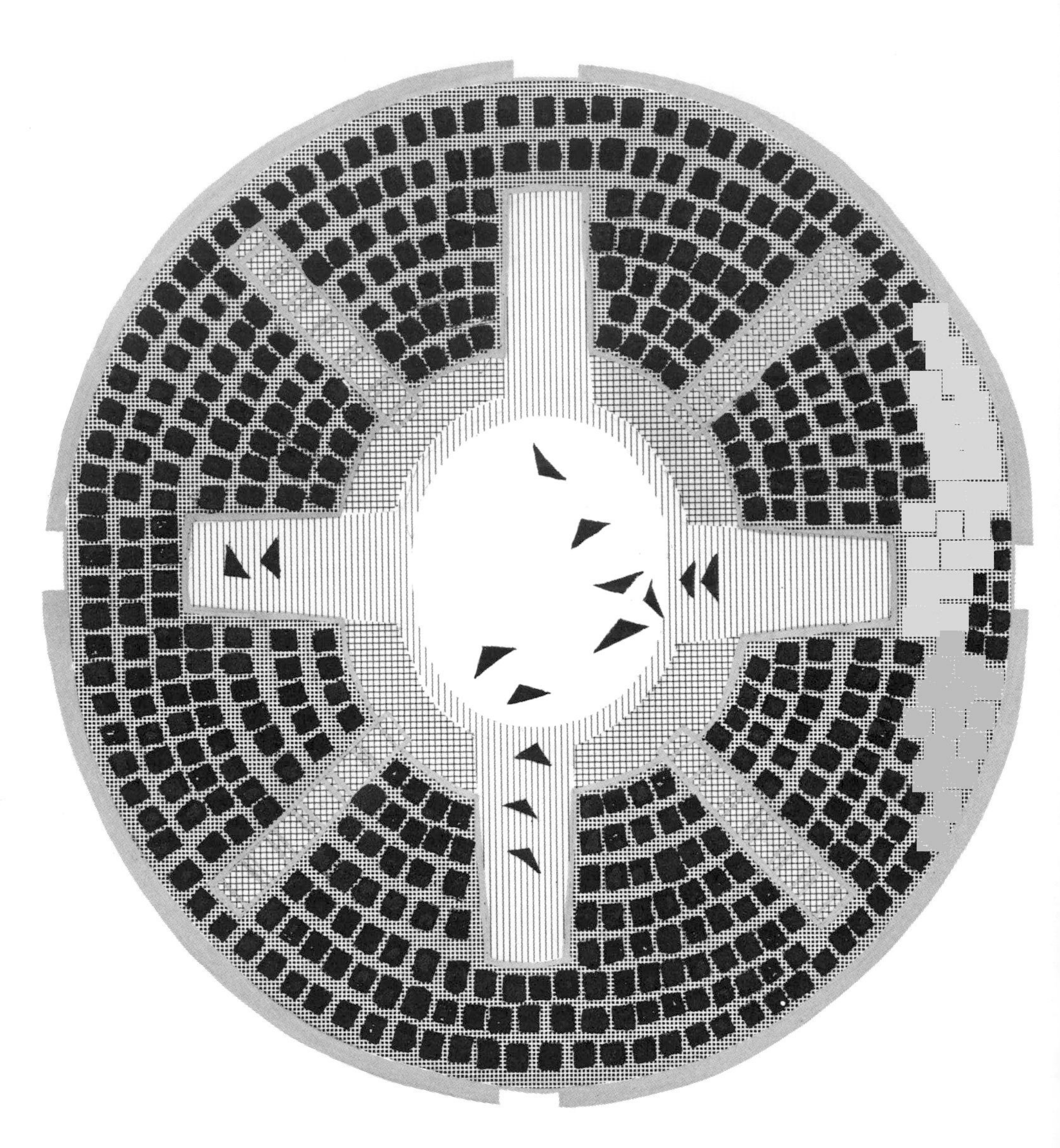

FIG. 52

FIG. 53

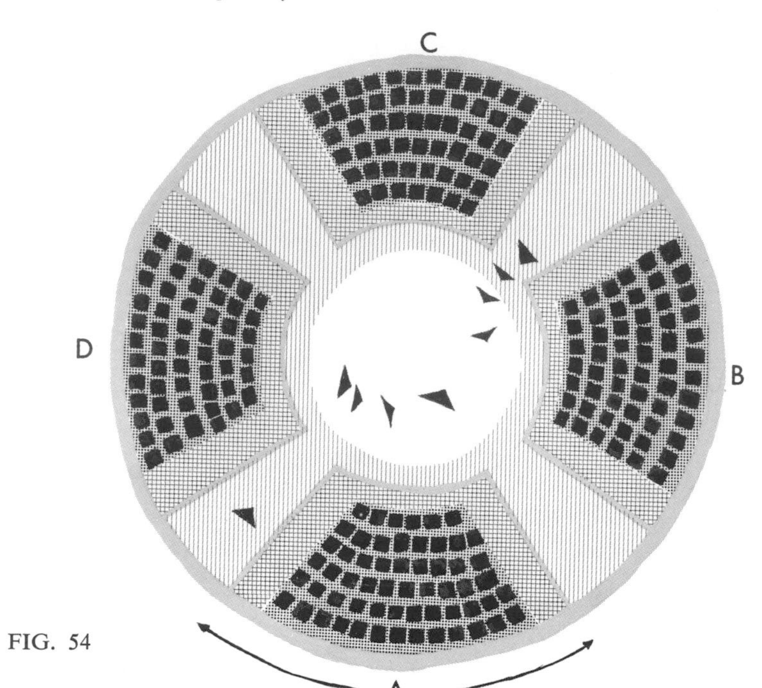

FIG. 54

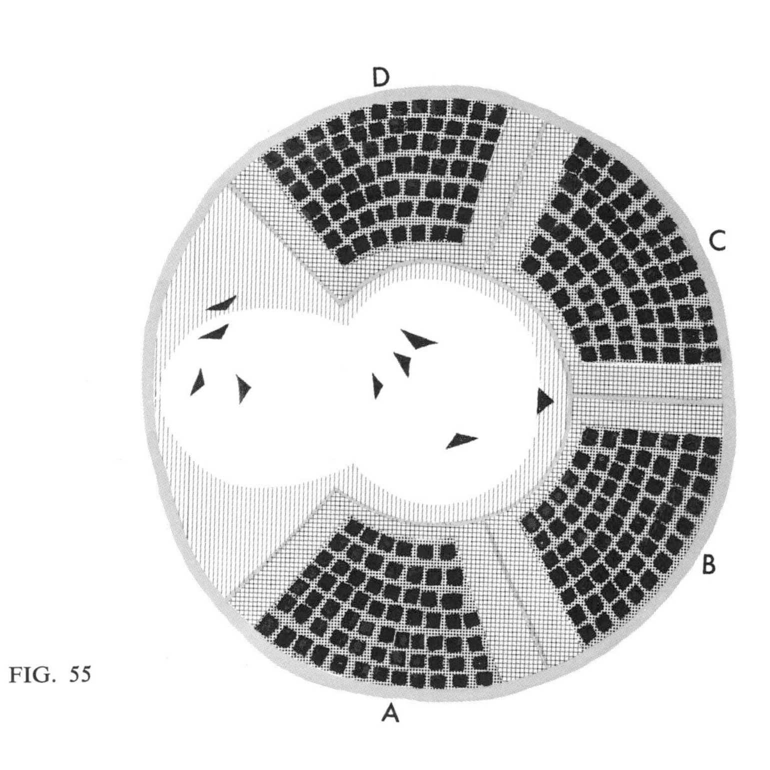

FIG. 55

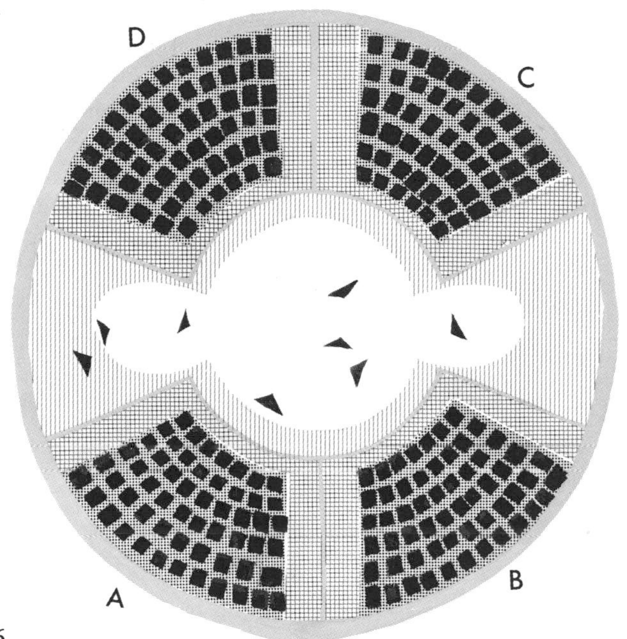

FIG. 56

Appendix

A List of Theatres Jo Mielziner Designed, Co-designed, and on Which He was a Consultant

One Astor Plaza 1968–1971 1,600-seat musical house	Times Square, N.Y.	Consultant to Albert Selden (who has lease) on seating sightlines on stage equipment on stage lighting Architects–Kahn & Jacobs
360° Theatre 1969 500-seat house	Project for a basement in a New York high rise building.	Total design by Jo Mielziner on seating sightlines on stage equipment on stage lighting
Porto Theatre 1966–1969 1,000-seat musical	Totally portable theatre–commissioned by the U.S. State Dept.	Total co-design with: Edward F. Kook Cyril Harris Donald Oenslager
Power Center 1964–1970 1,200 seats	Ann Arbor, Mich.	Co-designer with Architects–Roche, Dinkeloo & Associates on seating sightlines on stage equipment on stage lighting
University of Southern Illinois 1966–1970 1,200 seats	Edwardsville, Ill.	Co-designer with Architects–Hellmuth, Obata, & Kassabaum, Inc. on seating sightlines on stage equipment on stage lighting
Greenwich High School 1966–1967 750-seat theatre	Greenwich, Conn.	Designed the seating sightlines stage equipment stage lighting Architects–Reid & Tarics

National Life Theatre 1966 974 seats	Nashville, Tenn.	Co-designer with Architects—Skidmore, Owings & Merrill on seating sightlines on stage equipment on stage lighting
Loretto Hilton Center 1965 600 seats	Webster College, St. Louis, Mo.	Consultant on seating sightlines stage equipment stage lighting Architect—Theodore J. Wofford
Krannert Center 1964 1,200 seats	Champaign, Ill.	Consultant to Architect —Max Abramovitz on seating sightlines on stage equipment on stage lighting
The White House 1964	Washington, D.C. (portable stage for the East Room)	Total design and light- ing by Jo Mielziner
Steubenville College Theatre 1963 672 seats	Steubenville, Ohio	Co-designer with Joseph Bontempo (Architect) on seating sightlines on stage equipment on stage lighting
ANTA–Washington Square 1962 1,260 seats	Washington Square, N.Y.	Total design by Jo Mielziner seating sightlines stage equipment stage lighting
Dartmouth Theatre 1962 850 seats	Hanover, N.H.	Consultant to Architects —Harrison & Abramo- vitz
Mark Taper Forum 1961 750-seat theatre	Los Angeles Music Center	Co-designer of seating sightlines stage equipment stage lighting Architect—Welton Becket
Paradise Island Theatre 1959 1,500 seats	Nassau, B.W.I. Commissioned by Huntington Hartford	Co-designer with John L. Volk, Architect

Vivian Beaumont 1958–1965 1,250 seats	Lincoln Center, N.Y. Repertory Theatre	Co-designer with Architect Eero Saarinen on seating sightlines on stage equipment on stage lighting
Forum Theatre 1958–1965 299 seats	Lincoln Center, N.Y.	Co-designer with Architect Eero Saarinen on seating sightlines on stage equipment on stage lighting
La Jolla Repertory Theatre 1957	La Jolla, Cal. (design of stage only)	Co-designed: seating sightlines stage equipment stage lighting Mosher & Drew, Architects
5 Lincoln Square Theatres 1956 750–1,800 seats	Project commissioned by Roger Stevens	Co-designer with Architects Pererier & Luckman seating sightlines stage equipment stage lighting
Ziegfeld Theatre (Curtain for Billy Rose) 1955	New York, N.Y.	Designed by Jo Mielziner
Theatre Square (project only) 1952 1,250 seats	Los Angeles, Cal. Project commissioned by Huntington Hartford	Co-design with Architect Frank Lloyd Wright
Pan American Theatre 1950 2,000-seat musical & dining theatre	Dallas, Texas (for George Marshall) Pan-American Exp.	Total design by Jo Mielziner seating sightlines stage equipment stage lighting
Pittsburgh Playhouse 1949–1951 1,000 seats	Pittsburgh, Pa. Repertory Theatre	Designed: seating sightlines stage equipment stage lighting in collaboration with Charles & Edward Stotz

Index

NOTE: *Italic page numbers indicate illustrations.*